GW00865764

This book is dedicated to my mother
Winifred Jean Alleyne, S.R.N.

The following persons have made this undertaking
a pleasure. They have facilitated my effort
assiduously and unsparingly, have gone out of the
way of their normal duties to assist this venture; so
I have thought it fitting to make mention of these
hardworking people:

The staff at the Barbados Public Library;
Ms. Kurlyne Alleyne; Mr. Ezra Callender;
Mrs. Pauline Park-Mclaren;
Mr. Baba Elombe Mottley,
and
Ms. Carol Pitt of Caribbean Chapters Publishing.

First Edition, April 2017.

ISBN (paperback): 978-154-5107-56-0

Table of Contents

Disclaimer

This book is a memoir.
The events are portrayed to the best
of the author's memory.

The conversations in the book all
come from the author's recollections,
though they are not written to
represent word-for-word transcripts.
The author has retold them in a way
that evokes the feeling and meaning
of what was said, and in all instances
the essence of the dialogue is
accurate.

Extended Disclaimer

When I made the decision to write this book, I was in a quandary. Having read so many autobiographies before, I wanted something different from the usual. I wanted something entertaining, informative, and educational.

I've set out to tell my story with some footnotes, anecdotes and jokes to boost the entertainment quality, validate the information, and allow the educational side to be palatable to people of all ages.

I've made serious attempts at the above-mentioned. But if at any time I've failed to live up to my syllabus, please accept my humble apology.

If for any intent or purpose anything in this book offends you just remember that it wasn't done intentionally.

It would be remiss of me not to mention the people who have facilitated this venture. And so without further ado I will mention them, albeit briefly, as a preamble to my discourse.

Acknowledgements

First of all let me give praise to the Almighty God, for he has given me the ability to express myself in the written word even when mortal man has attempted to deny my opportunity to speak. So all praise is due to the Omnipotent One who has stayed with me from time immemorial and has kept me safe.

My father—a man I never knew—for donating the seed of his loins to intersperse with my mother's and allowing me to arrive. Thanks for not employing 'coitus interruptus' or using the now ever-popular condom, or else I might now be floating around the galaxy with the zillions of the unborn.

My mother, with whom I was only really close in her final months alive, even though I've never lived with anyone else for as long. Thanks for giving me as close as is humanly possible a father as any woman could endeavor to, and for guiding me to the right side of the road. Despite our many shortcomings you did a great job, and I am eternally grateful. My biggest regret is not being able to spend enough quality time with you as I did with Ma-Ma (my grandmother).

To my grandmother, the only person besides God Almighty who made me feel safe from harm and the deeds of evil men—the rock of my salvation. The time we spent together was short but intense. Unfortunately when you became ill for the final time, I also became sick and was only reunited in body with you at your funeral, one of the saddest days of my life. Ma-Ma I didn't become a lawyer or a doctor or any of the 'high-faluting' jobs that would have made you immensely proud, but one thing I've maintained throughout my sojourn here on this earth is the morsel of wisdom you imparted to me as a young boy. To maintain my dignity, I let no man lead me astray and any mistakes I made, I made them on my own, for then and only then would I be able to make my corrections. It is for this Ma-Ma that I dedicate this book to you wherever you are.

To my grandfather. Just like my father, I never saw you. You died long before I was born. But all through my life I've felt your presence, especially when confronted with danger, or when I was about to do something wrong. I guess that was the policeman in you looking out for your only grandson. Thanks Pa. I am eternally grateful. Thanks again.

To my adopted grandfather Mr. Ethelbert Heath— my guardian, my mentor, my helper and as so many said, my spoiler. Despite what the critics said (I never paid them any mind), no one knew you the way I did, and they never spent the amount of time we spent together. One thing I must respect you for is the way you adored my grandmother, and the way you cared for me, even though we were biologically unrelated. You were the one who insisted I take after-school lessons and you were the one who recommended Mr. Durant of Roebuck Primary to be my tutor. Thanks a million for allowing me the opportunity to acquire a top level education at two of the most wonderful and prestigious schools a person could hope to attend. Thanks Granddaddy, I appreciate your kindness immensely.

To my uncle David Alban Alleyne, after whom I was named. You were my disciplinarian. Without you I might have stumbled into so many degenerate misfits and ultimately be led astray. It was you who took me through every crack and crevice of 1960s Bridgetown city and showed me all the 'shituations' a disobedient boy could fall into.

I know you thought I was presumptuous, but I never strayed from your teachings. I can remember riding with you on your ladies' wheel bicycle, going to the movies or to get a haircut at Badenock's Barbershop off Brown's Beach, or going to Pebbles Beach and liming with you down by Cuz's. I swear every time I see a 7-Up sign or bottle your face flashes right before me. Honestly.

Of the others, let me mention Mr. Sampson of Bay Primary, my first official teacher; then Mr. Durant, my teacher after school; Mr. Harry Sealy was the greatest influence in my young life; Mr. Timothy Callender who discovered and aroused my interest in reading and creative writing.

Only God knows how much I miss you all. That's why I've travelled close to your teachings and exhortations my entire life. Suffice it to say that had I not encountered all of you in my time, I doubt that I could have been the man I am today.

To anyone I have omitted, it's not that I mean to be disrespectful, but the aforementioned have made such a significant contribution to my life that I must set them aside from anyone else.

As we travel along this concourse, there will be other persons whom I will mention, and their relationship with this man everyone knows as Scotty.

ONE LOVE.

A Brief History of Nelson Street

This discourse, for all intents and purposes, is a historical map for those who have never set foot or spent any length of time in Nelson Street. I have tried to use it to illuminate those who have been blindfolded by society's prejudices toward the area over the years.

I have used many real life characters and situations to highlight the everyday lives of these oftentimes scapegoated folks. They are normal, everyday people just like anyone else on the island. Some of the discrimination they have had to endure has been of their own making, but most of it I personally have found to be ill-founded.

Many so-called historians have attempted to write the area's history, but in my humble opinion they have come up quite short. They have failed to connect with the older ones who live there, and some I suspect have never been inside the place they love to call a haven for publicans and sinners.

These are doing a grave injustice to the many young children who through no fault of their own have to call this place their home. This propaganda has resulted in many of them becoming ostracized by their peers, and subsequently they lose interest in making any meaningful contribution to the country. Many of them feel as if they have marginalized by the stereotypical image with which they have been erroneously portrayed.

As in the case of Jewelina, many are debarred from the acquisition of certain types of work solely on the basis of their origins. This seems to be the exact same thing that black people the world over are crying out against. This comes as no surprise when the ones meting out this punishment are of the caucasian pigmentation. As a matter of fact, it is what one has come to expect from these people who look different from us.

But how can one stomach such uncouth behavior when it comes from your own kind, and from a people who suffer the same fate when in the land of the white man? One can never feel the heartache like these folks do when they can read a visitor advisory that proclaims Nelson Street as a 'no-go area' when on this fair island, and this advisory comes lock, stock and barrel from none other than the Tourist Board of the country.

Why should the many businesses in the area be made to suffer for what I perceive as nothing more than a historical blunder made by people who know nothing about the people they are criticizing?

Surrounded by the boundaries of River Road, Bay Street, Fairchild Street, Probyn Street and Jemmott's Lane, the Nelson Street enclave is criss-crossed by a network of roads and alleys. Contrary to popular belief, Nelson Street was not named in commemoration of the notorious Lord Nelson. The name derives from an eighteenth century resident and property owner.

Benjamin Harris, a resident of the area, was bequeathed a piece of land taken out of a parcel which had been bought from a Mr. Riding, and which had an adjoining piece owned by a Mrs. Nelson. This was described as land situated thirty feet from Nelson's corner, from thence a parallel line to Nelson's down to the swamp, and on to Nelson's lower corner.

The will for this was dated January 15 1756, two years before Admiral Viscount Nelson was born. After this the land in and around Nelson Street was owned by a certain Charles Sargeant. He had left directions that two years after his death all income accruing from the rental of his property was to go to the four children of his brother, William Sargeant. Thereafter the property itself was to go to the children of his sister Sarah Rebitt, the wife of a certain Peter Rebitt.

Events appear sketchy at this point, but what is divulged is that after Sergeant died, his brother's children sold their interests to Peter for sums each of five hundred pounds. In his will dated December 11 1821, Peter mentioned that William Oxley, the Master in Chancery, had prevented a sacrifice of Sargeant's property. In gratitude he made a request of one hundred and twenty pounds to Oxley's son and named two roads which had recently been cut through the land, Oxley Street and Chancery Lane.

As was previously mentioned, Nelson Street itself was a residential neighborhood as far back as the 18th century, but none of the streets which criss-crossed Rebitt's Land existed at the time. The first of these streets to be named was Wellington Street, that road which runs from Nelson Street to upper River Road.

Around 1858 Thomas Henry Rebitt, eldest son of the late Peter Rebitt, donated a strip of land in this area to the vestry of St. Michael to enable a right of way to be cut through to Bay Street. He was not the owner of the adjacent lands. This was the property of one Joseph William Bourne, the eldest son of London Bourne, a black businessman and planter. William Bourne, himself a planter, went bankrupt in 1862 and the following year a William P. Trimingham, the official assignee, sold 3,232 square feet of Bourne's land to the vestry to enable Wellington Street to be carried through to Bay Street.

The land adjacent to the said road which was originally part of Bourne's property is now owned by the Barbados government, and a housing project has been constructed there with the appropriate name of London Bourne Towers.

The Pondside, which lies just a little southwards, was part of the estate which the Rebitts inherited from

A view of modern day Nelson Street from Fairchild Street

Chancery Lane

View of Wellington Street from Bay Street

London Bourne Towers

The Pondside

St. Ambrose Church

Charles Sargeant. It owes its name to a large fish pond which was located on the spot, which some years ago was partially occupied by a garage at the junction of Waterloo Alley and Bay Street.

St. Ambrose Church was erected sometime in late 1857, and was consecrated on January 1st of the following year. A report taken from *The Barbadian* newspaper of March 1857 offers:

> "The Rev. Joseph S. Mayers, on his arrival from America, having been placed for a brief period in charge of St. Paul's District, saw at once that there was a need for a church—the adjoining church of St. Paul's accommodating 1,200 in a population of 13,000. The place known as Rebitt's Ground had in it an amount of spiritual destitution [that was] startling in the extreme, and covered with a pall of darkness too deep to be fancied, and only realized by those who have explored the area.
>
> "The place once the abode of filth, misery and vice; the scene of cockfights, dignities [balls] and other degrading dances; whose very atmosphere was polluted with the dreadful imprecation of the blasphemous, became an object of extreme solicitude to his mind."

Very strong language, but albeit also one very familiar to modern day ears. Remember, this was 1857. The land for the church was donated to the Lord

Bishop of Barbados by Thomas and Peter Rebitt. The money for its erection was raised through private contributions, loans and grants from the legislature, and by the proceeds of a bazaar. The cost of the building was £8,000, a handy sum in those days. It was designed by John Inniss, and the owner of Clapham Plantation donated the cornerstone.

Now we come to Jemmott's Lane, but first let me give you a word about Bay Street. The landward side of the road, up until the early 18th century, was devoted to agriculture. In January 1805 some 12 acres of land lying between Lower Bay Street and Jemmott's Lane were offered for sale for the building of houses. At the same time at Upper Bay Street several lots, each 100 ft. deep, were offered for sale.

Up until 1820 Jemmott's Lane had no name. It was merely described as the road that led to the place of execution of condemned criminals, this place of execution being Enmore on Collymore Rock. Jemmott's Lane was at first called Carlisle Lane, probably derived from the residence of Gabriel Jemmott (1761–1832) which stood on the grounds purchased in 1839 to house the General Hospital. Hence the road was named Jemmott's Lane some time after.

Probyn Street was named after Sir Leslie Probyn, Governor of Barbados (1911 – 1918). It was constructed under a plan for the improvement of Lower Bay Street following the fire of July 1910. It was the last street to be named after a British Governor. Jordan's Lane, named after Thomas Jordan, a property owner, originally extended to Bay Street, but the lower half became incorporated into Probyn Street.

Fairchild Street itself was named after Colonel John Fairchild who lived around the mid-18th century. He served many years on the vestry for the parish of St. Michael and was appointed Chief Justice in November 1752. He died in 1763.

Now a place of business, Fairchild Street was a residential area until early in the last century. Here, on May 14th 1854, a resident died under suspicious circumstances and within three days similar deaths occurred at nearby Nelson Street.

On the following day the Board of Health issued a notice stating that certain cases of a suspicious nature resembling Asiatic cholera had occurred in town, but there was no evidence to decide that the disease actually existed on the island. However, the disease soon spread from street to street, and by mid-June the epidemic had spread islandwide. By August 6th the known number of deaths was 15,243. The final death toll effected by this epidemic was officially recorded as 20, 727, one seventh of the total population of the island at the time. Some 9,127 of these were from the St. Michael and Bridgetown area.

The site of the former Harbor Police station on Bay Street was once the location of an institution called the 'Lock Hospital'—the Hospital for Contagious

Jemmotts Lane

The old General Hospital gate

The old Harbour Police entrance

The Fairchild Street market

Diseases as it was officially called.

In 1866, the British Government passed an Act for the prevention of Contagious Diseases at certain Naval and Military stations with the object of protecting members of the armed forces from venereal infection. The British Government had further offered to contribute 2,500 pounds towards the building of a hospital for the medical treatment of the "local ladies of the town" and an additional subsidy for the maintenance of 25 beds.

On July 30th, 1868 the Barbados Legislature passed a Contagious Diseases Act. A plot of ground was purchased at Bay Street and the hospital was erected in 1869 and opened on December 1st. The Act required the registration, compulsory medical examination and treatment, if necessary, of any woman reported as a suspected prostitute. Any woman who failed to report within seven days, who refused examination or treatment, or who being an inmate left the institution before having been discharged, was liable to be imprisoned for one month for the first offence, and three months for every subsequent offence

The hospital closed its doors in 1887 after the Contagious Diseases Act was repealed, and the following year the premises were allocated to the constabulary of the Harbor Police and the Fire Station which had hitherto been stationed at Combermere Street near the General Hospital.

River Road, that stretch of road that joins Fairchild

Street to Jemmott's Lane, was also a residential area, and ran alongside the Constitution River. This was actually an arm of the sea that ran some distance inland in high tide, sometimes as far as the Harmony Hall District.

Many will recall that whenever the dark and murky waters of the 'river' were disturbed an effluvium rose, giving off a pungent odor. Anyone causing this to occur was found guilty of contravening the Public Health Act of 1908. The Constitution River and the remnants of Bridgetown swamp were filled in during the year 1962 and was replaced with a canal. The nearby Pa Howell Spring would have to give way to the new Queen Elizabeth Hospital at Martindale's Road around the same time.

These then are the boundary lines of the Rebitts' Land, or 'Ground' as it was originally referred to, and Nelson Street. This is part of an area recently designated as a World Heritage Site. As reported before, this heritage is wrapped up in events mostly of a sinful and unfortunate nature. Therefore it can be seen how this legacy of ostracism and mistrust has permeated right through from the late seventeenth century until the present one.

Nevertheless, Nelson Street cannot be left out of any meaningful discussion on the history of Bridgetown. To do so would be to erase a major chunk of our national story. I dare say there are many who would endeavor to do such, if only to eliminate the folks of

Rebitt's land from their family album.

I have taken pains here to clearly outline the historical path the area has travelled in order to chart the one that lies ahead for the people of Nelson Street and their children. As no one else has undertaken this task, I have made it my duty to attempt to bring a better understanding of this simple area inhabited by hard-working, ambitious and talented folks who have been used for years as the whipping boys for a society that is quick to cast blame on the most vulnerable and disadvantaged in their midst.

Part One

Whores and Thieves

Some people claim that Nelson Street derived its name from the one-eyed, one-handed, notorious criminal whose replica stands outside the House of Assembly. Others (who I think are old enough to know) vehemently deny this. However, they have no claim to knowledge of the origins of the name except for the denial that Lord Nelson had nothing to do with the area. In fact, many have communicated to me that Nelson Street was once a place of respectable families and beautiful homes built along the Georgian and Victorian architectural styles of Great Britain.

As I traverse the area, I can bear witness to the validity of such arguments when I see some of these period constructs that have remained on the Nelson Street landscape. One such building that comes to mind is the New York Club. Recently refurbished, it has the trellises and other identifying features of Georgian 18th century wood and coral stone structures. Needless to say, in modern times this was converted into a brothel house. From the moment I had the opportunity to enter it I found an interior of such palatial proportions that the business proceedings taking place there seemed completely out of order.

Then there is Martineau House at the corner of Beckwith and Bay Street, where the Barbados Labor Party was founded. With its outlook loft surveying the pristine waters of Carlisle Bay, one can envision this as a residence of great importance in the days when Barbados ruled the Western Hemisphere as the bright shining jewel in the British Crown.

Further on Beckwith Street on the corner with Chancery there is another structure made of wood where renowned political statesman Wynter Crawford was born. This was called The American Club, but when I knew it, it was called simply 'Miss Darlington shop'. With its verandahs and residences on the top floor, completing the set was a rum shop downstairs that operates to the present day.

About fifty meters to the north there is another one-storied Georgian structure which went by the name of the Silver Dollar night club. This was another brothel. However, on close inspection, this building carried the same style of verandah as both The American Club and Martineau House. Only on this occasion this one was out fitted with a flag pole, from which the Union Jack was flown in colonial times.

The significance of these verandahs was brought home to me recently by author George Lamming. He said and I quote:

The Silver Dollar

Martineau House

MARTINEAU HOUSE
IN THIS BUILDING ON THE
SIXT DAY OF MARCH, 1938
THE BARBADOS LABOUR PARTY
HELD ITS FIRST MEETING.

THIS PLAQUE WAS ERECTED
IN CELEBRATION OF ITS
GOLDEN JUBILEE
BY THE CITY OF BRIDGETOWN
CONSTITUENCY BRANCH

"the people of the day built their chattel houses to define their positions or so-called positions in life. There were those with simple verandahs which were accessed by two steps and were mainly opened and were just an addition to the main house. Then there was the same verandah, but it was framed with jalousie windows. Now the owner of the second dwelling was seen to be of a higher standing than the owner of the first. Then there was the verandah that completely surrounded the structure and was also framed by jalousie windows. The owners of such a building would be seen to be of the nobility class. However, they all had one thing in common—poverty. Their houses were all built differently, but they were ultimately all poor."

Even in the lower-class areas of The Pondside (not the elaborate housing units, but its forerunner of derelict sub-human living quarters) there was a cock-loft similar in design if not in size to the one at Martineau House. Then there was The Exchange building on the site of the now London Bourne Towers. This was a coral stone structure at the corner of Bay and Wellington Streets, and was made along the Victorian style as were many of the buildings running along the roadside on Bay Street. It must be noted that in the colonial days the beach side to Bay Street was unoccupied by building structures, so

The American Club

The New York Club

all of the buildings on this side are of a more recent construct.

Going further back into the history of the area, I was informed that the place we now refer to as Nelson Street was called 'Phoenix City' by the locals. Later the name of Rebitts Land was given in recognition of the original owners of the area. The title of Rebittarian was given to any one whose navel string was buried in there.

It is against this historical background that I now set up the theatre of my thesis. On the one hand there was Nelson Street proper with its stately mansions of the day occupied by the nobility and semi-aristocrats; a scenario far removed from the debauchery and blatant vulgarity that now lends itself to modern day Nelson Street. On the other hand there was the plantation tenant of the Rebitts with their residents emerging from the poorer classes of the day.

Somewhere along the way a paradigm shift occurred, probably catalyzed by the coming to prominence of the naval culture of Carlisle Bay, and growing cravings of the merchant and navy seamen of early 19th century Bridgetown.

These needs were satisfied by the many 'hotels'—for want of a better term—that sprung up on the landscape, and the 'ladies' who were called upon to soothe the lustings of these 'gentlemen' in ways unbecoming of women of grander upbringing. This is of a similar nature to what now lends itself on Nelson

Street today.

Now we see a pattern forming here. Whereas in former times Nelson Street was an area for the rich and respectable, it now has been transformed over a period of time into a haven of carnal behavior. And where Rebitts Land had earlier carried that same characterization, now the inhabitants thereof had become for the most part church-going and humble hard-working individuals. The train of occupation had been set in motion.

Many a weary sailor, after landing on Barbadian soil, would have become intoxicated by the local grog and ultimately desired more than his fair share of the female attention without the attending fee. Therefore it would have been logical to employ some strong-armed roughnecks to defend these fair damsels, as well as bring some semblance of order in the absence of the local constabulary.

Anyone who is even vaguely familiar with these establishments would know this can be a very dangerous occupation, not one for the faint of heart or one who has a fear for the sight of blood. Needless to say many a sailor might have ended up on the losing side, as he would inevitably be fighting against opponents of greater numbers and who more importantly were on their own home soil. It does not take a Solomon to surmise that any bounty carried by these battered and sea-worn men would have been taken as prize money for the efforts of these hired henchmen. Not to mention any amorous favors the 'ladies' could offer as means of appreciation for the much needed chaperoning by these 'bad-johns'.

In the present time the game is played a little differently. The existing laws present prostitution as an illegal event in Barbados, and the emergence of human trafficking involving the likes of Guyanese, Santo Domingans and Jamaicans, etc., the police and immigration combine to intercede and interrupt anyone caught in there. Today this activity is no longer hushed and swept under the proverbial rug. It has now become a crime, and many are now convicted on such offences as allowing one's premises to operate as a brothel, along with the earlier mentioned one of human trafficking.

It is from such a theatre that the humble folks of Nelson Street and its environs have had an ignoble title thrust upon them by the rest of the island. Whores and thieves!

Rumshopology

As mentioned before, Barbados has an abundance of watering holes. Tradition lends to the existence of these establishments primarily for the function of recreational and habitual drinking. Socialisation is of a lesser concern to the more hardened drinker, and of more concern to the working class in search of a meeting point or an opportunity to let off steam.

From as early in the morning as can be conceivable, many can be found outside the doors of the rum shop waiting anxiously and feverishly for its opening. The hardcore drinker would usually forget his breakfast meal and replace it with a shot of rum.

As copious quantities of the beverages are imbibed, the effect of the drug-like symptoms can become clearly evident. Slurring of speech, vociferous dialogue, a propensity for colorful language and a general sense of false euphoria are the trademark signs of the inebriated.

The topics of the day are generally debated under such conditions, with the result that sometimes heated discussions turn into personal squabbles and the combatants relinquish reason and rationale, replacing it with character-bashing and denigration, in complete divergence from the original moot of the discussion.

Needless to say many of these squabbles can easily become volatile and turn into psychical skirmish. More often than not the law officials have to be summoned to break up fights, restore order, or in some extreme cases cart some unfortunate individual or individuals off to the local precinct to cool off, or in the case of the more severe instance of wounding, creating a disturbance, or God forbid murder/manslaughter, brought before the law courts.

Despite these challenges, dangerous as they may seem, the rum shop, in its peaceful element, especially when patronized by the more socially equipped and intelligent kind of drinker, can be a venue for thrashing out the issues of the day.

The bartender, usually the proprietor, takes on the role of the Speaker of the House of Assembly in this Westminster political divide. Normally unbiased and non-partial, he is the sole arbitrator of any verbal spats likely to occur. His wisdom is presumed. His counsel is validated by his right of privilege. He is the one who controls the elixir. Many an argument can be settled by the bartender, especially if he issues a round of drinks on the house so that for some time peace can reign, until the next topic arises.

Topics in the rum shop can emerge fast and furious, sometimes quicker than the time it takes for Usain Bolt to complete the 100 meters dash. It only depends on the level of intoxication and the adrenalin pumping at the time. Cricket, football, politics, medicine, music, government issues, the cost of living—all these usually run the gamut of rum shop debates.

The rum shop can also become a place of learning and enlightenment, a source of comic relief, and a forum for raising discussion on social development and community relations. In the absence of a Community Human Resource Centre, the rum shop acts as a viable interface between community members and political representatives.

It is the place where marriages are made and broken, where jobs are gained and lost, where rumors are started and then dispelled, and love affairs are concealed and revealed. In other words, the rum shop carries its own laws of relativity to balance the scales of life or sometimes tip them in the wrong direction. Many friendships are ruined by gossip and a system of psychological bullyism whereby the bigger spender can muster support against a drinker of lesser financial status, solely on the basis that the piper calls the tune.

One incident that comes to mind occurred during an election time when the ruling party at the time seemed under pressure to lose control of the majority. Many public workers who happened to frequent a particular rum shop on Nelson Street were up in arms a couple of days before election day, in order to garner support for the government of the day. Needless to say rum was flowing, discussions were heated, and the rum pimps were having a field day.

One worker, on inviting some pimps to a drink, started to canvass against the opposition as soon as the opening rituals of passing out the plastic cups started, and then the breaking of the seal culminating in the pouring of the 'sacrament', whereupon one rum pimp was heard to say:

"Yeah man, my vote strictly for the DLP, in full respect to my man Errol Barrow," mentioning one of Barbados' National Heroes and the man known as the 'Father of Independence'. "Don't mind he dead and gone, Barrow works will always live on."

And the gathering raised their glasses in salutary toast, knocked them together and each one threw back their heads and in unison 'knocked back' a shot of rum. Then in turns they poured water to chase the fire water. The government worker, believing that his work had been completed, at least in this particular establishment, announced his intention to take leave and everyone present reassured him of their support for the DLP in the coming elections.

Minutes later, after the first bottle had expired, the rum pimps relapsed into their innocuous state of lethargy and awaited the arrival of more liquid benevolence. This came in the form of a bus driver for the National Transport Board, who was clearly dissatisfied with the way things were being run by the present government. In no uncertain terms he made his feelings known and relayed his displeasure to all and sundry. The rum pimps, sensing fresh prey, sized up their man with speedy resolve and launched their assault.

"Yeah man! We need a change, things can't continue this way. Barrow dead and gone long time ago."

These were the same rum pimps who had earlier pledged their undying support for Errol Barrow's legacy and the ruling DLP.

"I does hate to hear people talking 'bout Barrow, Barrow, Barrow, like if he is God or something."

By now the entire shop had become engrossed in this exercise of political somersaulting.

"Owen is the man for me. I going with Owen." The rum pimp opined. And with that the unsuspecting bus driver handed him a bottle of newly purchased rum and replied:

"You are a man after my own heart, hit one ah dese rums with me."

The rum pimp, with a glint in his eye, accepted and turned to one of his buddies sitting close by and whispered:

"Yuh see, man yuh got to be flexible, yuh got to know how to live."

"Who kill de sailor?"

It was the seventies in Barbados. Some referred to it as the roaring seventies. Bridgetown was a buzz of activity, commercially and politically. Just four years into independence and national sovereignty, the people were now getting used to running their own affairs. It was a time when Barbados was beginning to make strides internationally before the United Nations.

The Prime Minister of the day, the Rt. Hon. Errol Barrow, had just made his famous 'friends of all and satellites of none' speech at the Security Council. The country had its first native Governor General, Sir Winston Scott, and the Hon. Ernest Deighton Mottley was the mayor of Bridgetown, a position of the same pomp and ceremony as the Governor General's.

With the achievement of independence and sovereignty, rapid strides were seen to be made in education and the Barbadian society began to demand higher standards of proficiency as well as transparency in all sectors of social and economic activity.

Up in St. Lucy the US naval base facility was in full effect (despite all the satellite talk by Barrow) and huge warships floating into Barbados on a daily basis were the order of the times. The Bridgetown Port and the Careenage with its inner basin transacted a bustling trade and many inter island-schooners and other vessels were plying their cargo into the main city of the island, minus the stringent regulations now in place, and immigrants from the nearby St. Lucia, Dominica and to a lesser extent St. Vincent had started arriving to trade and subsequently reside.

Many young men had started their occupational career as merchant seamen. Recruitment was done mainly in the city areas such as Chapman Lane, New Orleans, Nelson Street and the Bay Land. These now had a chance to experience life in the outside world and returned to Barbados not only clothed in the latest fashions and jewelry of the day, but also with some revolutionary concepts about the rights and privileges of their new country.

Both the Empire and Plaza Cinemas were showing the latest serving of violence and gore in the form of the Italian Westerns, James Bond and several other gladiator and pre–historic movies. Television was now becoming a novelty and everyone was aspiring to become the owner of one of these 'blind boxes'. The movie shows of the day were violent in their offerings and indeed the movie houses themselves were on occasion deemed to be dangerous places to go. Bottle throwing was almost a daily occurrence, and the Chapman Lane versus the Pine feud was boiling at the surface.

The late Jackie Opel had returned from Jamaica sporting a new hairstyle, prompting many to refer to him as a madman and a drug addict. He had brought with him a new beat he had invented while in Jamaica, and the word 'spouge' was on every lip on the island. The Bay Street esplanade was the stomping ground of the local artists of the day and many overseas talent also appeared there, including The Mighty Sparrow, Byron Lee and the Dragonaires, Fab Four, and a group from the land of reggae called Tomorrow's Children. They had a hit song at the time called *Mister Poor Man*. This was a song that every Nelson Street dweller could certainly relate to.

> *Passing down some crowded place*
> *They see him come and they turned their face*
> *No one cares about his life*

These are some of the lyrics of that song and it truly epitomized the plight of the average Nelsonian.

Nelson Street was a cohobblopot* of cultures at the time, as along with the small islanders there were some Haitians and Dominicans who were throwing their hats into the prostitution ring. The visiting sailors who hailed from America, the United Kingdom, and Germany frequented the area in pursuit of these sweet

---

* cohobblopot
  a mixture of something (like a meal) with a wide variety of ingredients

island ladies, and the night club scene was just about to take off in full force.

There was the Caribbean Pepperpot owned by Mr. Darnley Greenidge; the Zanzibar, run by Mr. Sydney Goddard; the New York Club controlled by Mr. Tonic Prescott; and then there was Harry's Nitery under the proprietorship of the imposing figure of Mr. Harry Wills; and there was the more prestigious Bel Air Jazz Club operated by Mr. Slims Giddens. Here a small jazz band would perform on a nightly basis and it would be commonplace to see such luminaries as Nina Simone, Mick Jagger, Elton John, Mr. George Drummond (who was said to be related to Her Majesty the Queen), and sometimes even the Rt. Hon Errol Walton Barrow would make a late night appearance.

Musical servings were of the highest order with such acts as Mr. Ernie Small (a resident of Queen's Street in the area), Ebe Gilkes, Mike Sealy, and that great guitarist Mr. Clifton Glasgow along with his protégé Mr. Julian Peters, and many a visitor would hop on the house piano and deliver an impromptu jam session, all backed by the Bel air Jazz band which boasted of the eighth wonder in the world—Tiddles, the sleeping drummer. Tiddles could keep time. No matter how many times they changed the tempo, he would be right there with the rest of the band, all the while perfectly at peace in a deep sleep.

Among the youth of Nelson Street there were the 'have's, mainly the offspring of the seamen, who were

The old Bel Air Jazz Club on Bay Street

in possession of all the latest toys and clothing their fathers could lug through the Bridgetown Harbour, and they generally wanted for nothing. Then there were the 'have-nots', the children of Bajan and St. Lucian amalgamations, and these were of the poorer sections of the area. The latter carried a disposition that betrayed their anger and frustration. Many were wont to pilfer the crates of mangoes and oranges that lay unattended during the night and many raids were secretly carried out to help placate the surging pangs of hunger experienced by many of these youngsters.

In those days serious crime was the mainstay of only a few and these convicts, as was said in those days, "all knew their cell number."

However, the streets were breeding a new kind of deviant, made into a dangerous piece of humanity by the socio–economic scramble he and his family found themselves immersed in—street kids with a difference. These would think nothing of snatching the bag of a tourist in the hope of being the bread winner for his hapless family. Indeed many parents secretly encouraged their charges to go looking for that bounty of the Yankee dollar bill, but were seen to publicly reprimand them if they were caught. Such was the corruption and confusion of the period that the streets were a dangerous place to be at nights for the uninitiated and street foolish.

The prostitutes did a rip roaring trade in those days—or nights—with the visiting sailors, and many a liaison had facilitated the emergence of little half-caste babies who were referred to as 'sailor children'. Clearly identifiable by their mainly caucasian features and pigmentation, they were ridiculed to some extent as to the origins of their fathers, and many of them carried themselves as if in possession of very low self-esteem, while others became deviants to society. Still, a minority placed all this drama behind them and set out to live positive and productive lives.

The poorer boys formed themselves into groups, or as they say today, gangs, each one armed with the popular Okapi ratchet knives which they used to identify themselves by, incessantly flicking them in public, much to the chagrin and horror of the passers-by. The police watched with an eagle eye, and waited to pounce at any given time on these villains. But they were speedy both on foot and on bicycle.

Guys like Roughhouse and Derrick, Numps, Patrick Barriteau and John 'Pemment' Marshall ruled the roost from the cinemas to the streets. Then there were their female companions, young ladies such as Magdalena, Lisha, and Audrey, who offered themselves as distractions for these early thugs.

On the other hand there were the grown men like Desmond Bump, Benjie the 'little short man', 'big ignorant Norman Edwards', and Cuthbert who also went by the name of Isaac Hayes because of his uncanny likeness to the movie star of the same name. These were an imposing sight for many a pedestrian on Nelson Street, day or night. They were usually well-dressed and had the financial backing of the whores of the day. These men supplied the security for the ladies in return for sexual favors and monetary drawbacks. In the United States of America these men were known by the derogatory name of 'pimp'. In Nelson Street, these were the 'Sweet Boys'.

It is easy to imagine the atmosphere that pervaded Nelson Street at that time. In those days it was called 'the street that never sleeps' long before the neighboring Baxter's Road had acquired the title. One could stand at one end of Nelson Street and look straight down to the other enjoying the acrobatic neon lights as they danced across the shop fronts, just like on the streets of Las Vegas. The juke boxes blasted the top twenty tunes of the day as the ladies would work their flirt in an effort to gain the attention of the naval men.

Some misinformed person or persons had probably told the sailors that, owing to the fact that they were for the most part of European descent, the island was their playground and the general populace were there solely at their beck and call. This attitude took root whenever these sea rovers imbibed too much of the local brew and became intoxicated to the point of irrational behavior. In such instances fights were rife. The military police had their work cut out as they tried desperately to maintain law and order amongst their colleagues.

On one such occasion a group of English sailors became embroiled in a heated exchange with the homeboy thugs. The discussion carried on much longer than it really should have, and boosted by the ever-rising levels of testosterone, neither side showed any intention of backing down.

After a while sledging words gave way to psychical contact and ultimately a scuffle ensued. The local thugs, not to be upstaged on their turf, swelled their numbers and armed themselves with broken bottles and knives of varying sizes and sharpness. The sailors, being the military men they were, sized up the situation and decided to withdraw and retreat from this theatre of violence, unintentionally leaving behind one of their own.

Over the years the facts surrounding this incident

have either been stretched to the limit, or changed around to protect the guilty parties involved, depending on who it was relating the story. For what eventually occurred took place in the dead of night and the darkest of alleys. Only those directly involved would be in a position to pinpoint the one who delivered the fatal blow or blows. The end result was one dead sailor. Not only that, but a dead sailor from Her Majesty's Queen Elizabeth of England's Royal Navy.

The next day the law enforcers began their investigations into the matter and many of the thugs and their girlfriends were taken into custody for questioning.

Rumor has it that, coerced by near fatal beatings from the police and with the fear of the ever-present hangman's noose dangling precariously over their heads, many a so-called hardened criminal had buckled and begun to sing like cuckoo birds. The result was that certain members of the gang turned into Crown's evidence, and fingers were pointed at one man—John 'Pemment' Marshall.

In a country where white is might and always right, the death of a white person can result in the native people calling for the blood of one of their own to quickly appease the families and relatives of the deceased. Public opinion would be heavily stacked against the black perpetrator regardless of the circumstances surrounding the incident.

No one from outside the area gave a damn how wrong the sailors were in their disrespect for the local residents, or how right the thugs were for acting as vigilantes against these marauding instruments of war who were now posing as humble peace-makers. The island called for the execution of one of their sons in much the same way the Jews called for Jesus to be crucified and Barabas to be exonerated.

Nelson Street was divided, as many voiced their concerns for the youngsters and their violent activities. Many called for all of them to be executed to serve as a lesson to the delinquency and deviant behavior that had reared its ugly head on the streets of Bridgetown. Others sided with the thugs, for they were only, as they saw it, reacting to provocation enacted by a set of rowdy sailors who wouldn't have given any thought to wrecking the entire town and then leaving the Navy to foot the bill.

There was even sympathy from some of the night club owners who had experienced altercations with the said sailors, and had had to foot their own bill when the ship in question made an early exit before they could lodge a complaint. Needless to mention the trial was of great interest to the nation at large, and the press had a field day not only reporting the case as it unfolded, but they also took the opportunity to take some unnecessary swipes at the entire area of Nelson Street and its environs.

It was said that Nelson Street people were like

cannibals and pirates, and one newspaper columnist had labeled the area 'The Spanish Main', probably in reference to the many youths clad in bandana scarves and flicking their ratchet knives in symphony on the various street corners. Later this label was romanticized and shortened to 'The Main'.

Meanwhile, when judge and jury had deliberated, John 'Pemment' was found guilty of murder and sentenced to hang by the neck until dead. In a subsequent twist of events he was exonerated and his sentence commuted to life imprisonment (35 years) which he has served out, and has re-entered society no worse for wear. He has converted to the Christian faith and, having learnt his lesson, is currently working as a self-employed carpenter and joiner, trades he picked up during his time spent at Glendairy Prison.

Of the others, Rough House, who was initially suspected of killing the sailor, continued on his thug life path until he too was sentenced to hang for a murder he claimed he knew nothing about. He too was subsequently exonerated and has re–entered social life. The going has not been easy for Rough House as the years have not been kind to him, and now a mere shadow of his former self, he lives in perpetual fear that one of his victims of the past would someday recognize him and exact vengeance against him.

Derrick, on the other hand, met a fate of his own design. Having lived as a closeted homosexual for most of his life, he finally came out just in time to collide with the dreaded HIV/AIDS pandemic and became one of the early fatalities of the disease.

Numps now goes by the name Iration, in keeping with his conversion to the Rastafarian faith, and he too is advancing in age with some degree of disability.

Patrick Barriteau, a loose cannon at the time, fled to his native Grenada and joined the revolution there, becoming a member of the Maurice Bishop New Jewel Movement. He still resides there as far as I know.

Fortune has been kinder to the ladies.

Magdalena, after years of hustling and experiencing one traumatic relationship after another, finally lost her nerve one night and doused her abusive lover from head to foot with acid. Her victim refused to bring any charges against her in the hope of reconciling with her. She would have none of it, and fled to live on her own under the protection of her two teenaged sons. One night while working on the streets she met a rich white man, something she had sought after for many years. This man lavished all he could afford upon this beautiful specimen of a Negro woman. She now travels between Barbados, St. Lucia and Europe.

Audrey, the companion of Rough House, just like Magdalena, met a Swedish gentleman who took her to Sweden to live. Whenever she visits the island she never fails to seek out Rough House and provide him with whatever he needs. Rough House has an affinity for Audrey's two children even though they were born in Sweden and could only have heard about him from their mother.

Lisha is a newspaper vendor for one of the two local journals, and leads a productive life.

These are different times, and many of the players in this scenario have undergone change. They are now productive citizens for the most part who now lament of the errant ways of today's youth, probably forgetting their own days of rebellion. All in all, it matters little who killed the sailor. Only God can judge that now, but some good has come from the whole exercise.

Some tragedy has come about as well. Norman Edwards lost his life on a motorcycle he was ill-equipped to handle.

Desmond Bump was savagely attacked on board a ship by a Jamaican seaman and for years he held a grudge against anyone and anything Jamaican. His resentment of Jamaicans was carried forward to include the Rastafarians of Nelson Street, and he set out to wage a one-man war against the innocent brethren. The Brethren refused to be bullied, and Bump was ambushed one night and beaten into submission by the 'Nyah-Men'.

Benjie fell victim to the crack cocaine culture and became addicted to the substance and all its peripheral activities. His life descended from a series of lows to his untimely demise in unknown circumstances. His body was identified in the morgue of the Queen Elizabeth Hospital after being missing for many weeks.

The stories have been told; the lives have been lived and lost. Now the survivors are making the best of their lives considering the skeletons left in their closets.

As to who said what, why they said it, what they said, and who contributed the most to Pemment's arrest while under police interrogation, is now down to mere conjecture. And still to this day, more than forty years later, no one can clearly give answer to the question: "Who kill de sailor?"

The Coming of Dread

When Desmond Bump and the Sweet boys ruled the roost on Nelson Street in the late sixties and early seventies The Main was a melting pot of Caribbean cultures and lifestyles.

These were the days of the speculators and itinerant island travelers who moved from island to island seeking their fortunes by trading in their agricultural produce and hand-crafted household implements. These travelers came from St. Lucia, Dominica, St. Vincent, Guiana, the Dominican Republic and Haiti, with a much smaller helping coming from Trinidad and Jamaica.

The Barbadians referred to them, somewhat erroneously, as 'foreigners'. The visitors who hailed from much further away i.e. North America, United Kingdom and Canada, were simply known as tourists.

The St. Lucians were reputed to have entered the country as part and parcel of the burgeoning fruit trade. They were said to have arrived amongst the crated citrus cargo. Bajans never forgot to remind them that they came here in a mango crate marked 'Handle with care. This side up'.

Their patois, incomprehensible to the average Bajan whenever they spoke it, was thought it to be a weapon the Lucians were using in retaliation to their taunts. However, these St. Lucians were, to my knowing, very polite, hard working, industrious and giving, despite all the harassment they received. They knew how to enjoy themselves without causing rancor, and loved to party to their Cadance music the slightest chance they got.

Many of my young days were spent among these Lucians. It was they who translated every single word of Sparrow's *Sa Sa Ay*, informing me that had the authorities known the full meaning of these salacious lyrics, that song would never have seen the light of day on the local airwaves.

The Dominicans were similar in approach to the St. Lucians, and like them were mainly of the Catholic persuasion. They too spoke patois with great flourish. They too traded in citrus and coals, and they set up shops around their homes and in the nearby Fairchild Street market. These were another hardworking, respectful and entertaining lot.

The Vincentians were a quiet set of people, as they still are. Mainly of the Spiritual Baptist faith, they possessed a sense of spirituality that was not readily seen among the Lucians or the Dominicans. This kept them apart from the other small islanders in that they were devout religionists and their only bouts of public display were in their 'tie-head' revivalist meetings, where they entered the power of the Holy Spirit and chanted their praises unto their Creator. They too enjoyed some success at trading and were for the most part generally industrious.

Of the others, the Haitians and the Santo Domingans, because of their inherent features and natural beauty, the females took to the prostitution trade like proverbial ducks to water.

The wheels of the rip-roaring night club flesh trade were properly set in motion, and had begun to pick up momentum. It now became a necessity to import more ladies of the night to accommodate the night club scene, and along with readily available Haitians and Dominicans there were also some Lucians along with a smattering of Bajans.

Between the in-transit sailors and the longer staying tourists, Nelson Street became a bustling metropolis. It was one of the busiest streets in the Southern Caribbean. Here could be found grocer shops, bakeries, barber shops, drug stores, blacksmith shops and laundries which complimented the many rum shops and brothels to complete the commercial versatility of the area.

Making money was the order of the day, and US currency flowed like milk and honey in the Promised Land. Even small urchins such as myself would earn a small fortune by acting as a gopher for the sailors. We would be remunerated with a fifty cents piece that would all but make our day considering the state of the cost of living in those days.

Jackie Opel, a.k.a. Dalton 'Man Face' Bishop, had arrived from Jamaica and had brought with him the now ever popular dreadlocks hairstyle. Short as they were, this style stunned and shocked the usually conservative-minded Barbadian. The fact that these were achieved by ultimately refusing to cut or comb one's hair made it even more abhorrent to the normally well-groomed Bajan populace.

A Guyanese seaman who had espoused a Barbadian young lady, who in turn bore him two lovely children, stepped into the picture with a slightly aggravated version of the dreadlock style. His were of shoulder length and when coupled with his long beard gave him the appearance of a Black Jesus. He was Mikey Zephurin, and he would school Jackie in his performance routines that amazed audiences the world over.

Marijuana was used by a minority at the time, and only a privileged few knew of its potency and calming effects. In those days if you were even remotely suspected of partaking of the Holy herb, the stereotype of dope addict was immediately assigned to you.

All this took Nelson Street by storm, and quite a few converts, mainly of the younger set, sprang up outfitted with a generous growth of 'natties', and with their youthful looks garnered the attention of the more adventurous ladies of the night who sought some companionship with those lurking on the fringes of social life, as they themselves were, and who possessed a penchant for danger while flouting the laws of the land.

At this point Rastafarianism was about image alone. Theology and concept, even though already espoused by the brethren of Jamaica, was virtually unknown here at this time. The only tenet being that Emperor Hailie Selassie I the first of Ethiopia, who had earlier visited the island, was proclaimed as God Almighty.

In Barbados, a landscape dotted with rum shops, churches, cane fields, and police stations, a theory such as this was tantamount to blasphemy. This gave lawmen the perfect excuse to pursue the prosecution of these 'madmen' and to locate them within the confines of Jenkins, the local psychiatric hospital. Many Rastas had this punishment dished out to them solely for having the courage of their convictions to openly practice their religion.

All incidences of praedial larceny was blamed upon the non-meat-eating Rastas. This resulted in constant police harassment, and the society was up in arms with the lawmen to rid the country of this blight that threatened to befall their own offspring. No heed was paid to the philosophical and theological arguments of the 'Iyah-men' of the day. All that was perceived were a set of dope smoking, insane, unkempt blasphemers who played drums all day and all night, singing trance-like mantras in praise of a black King in Ethiopia.

This was the coming of 'dread' to Barbados, a time far removed from the attitudes and anniversaries that now obtain in present day Barbados, where the possibility of one day being ruled by a dreadlocked Prime Minister is just but a breath away, as indeed the present president of the Upper Chamber is a dreadlocked young lady. Another is a minister of Cabinet, one young lady who holds an opposition seat, as well as a few prominent lawyers. Most of these wear the dreadlocks as a style and have no religious binding of any sort to the faith.

One thing that endeared the Rastas to the Barbadian public was their surprisingly skilful application of leathercraft and other arts. They could be depended on to build a stronger pair of sandals than could be bought from any of the department stores in Bridgetown. They proceeded to set up their own mini shoe factory, albeit in the wrong commercial location, Rockers Alley, right next to Cave Shepherd on Broad Street. It was only a matter of time before this bubble would burst. Here was a group of ganja smoking, long-haired black men mass-producing footwear in the middle of town, and at a cheaper price than all of the leading stores.

Needless to say shoe sales at Cave Shepherd were completely obliterated. All that was needed was a perfect excuse to curtail this entrepreneurial venture. This came in the form of many complaints of harassment and incidences of bag snatching by members of the general public, all emanating from the confines of Rockers Alley. The perpetrators were castaways and low-life, petty thieves who daily infiltrated the ranks of the brethren to acquire a smoke and a sipping of ital food.

To cut a long story short, one afternoon the Babylonians arrived at Rockers Alley in full force and proceeded to 'suss out' the brethren, who immediately showed their displeasure by openly retaliating against the lawmen. A large crowd gathered and the situation turned ugly as it became clear that the brethren were not going to be allowed to walk away scott free, after administering such a clout to the face of the lawmen.

That was the orchestrated end of the Rastas on Broad Street. After a great hue and cry from mainstream Barbados the brethren were shunted into virtual obscurity to the nearby Temple Yard. This proved later to be a dangerous move, as an Electrical Power Station was located right in the centre of the market place. The brethren were moved once again, this time in the interest of their own safety. They were moved further down the commercial ladder to Cheapside, where they remain to this present day. However, they never regained the popularity and business that they possessed at Rockers Alley. I guess that the initial desired result was finally obtained.

All this occurred without any assistance from the Jamaicans, who were the original conceptualizers of the faith in the first place.

The popularity of Rastafarianism came about first because of the fervent religiosity of the average Barbadian, and secondly due to the growing frustration and mistrust of the accepted Church of the day. If Jackie Opel could start such a trickle, Bob Marley was sure to bring an avalanche with his lion-mane dreadlocks and prophetic teachings of Pan-Africanism and message of hope for the poor and disenfranchised. His open and militant opposition to traditional and colonial mores prompted the authorities to prohibit his entry into this last bastion of slavery, as it was felt his mere presence on the island would have had the same effect as Jesus' second coming .

But fast forward to the present, where dancehall artists are openly promoting slackness and profanity, homophobia and gun violence in an attempt to distort the mind set and value systems of the young and vulnerable. Alas, these performers are allowed free and full passage into Barbados, at this time to further corrupt and retard the youth of this fair isle.

Part Two

The Wild Boys and Their Toys

Bajan conservatism was probably instituted by the planters of the day as a salutary recognition of their Anglo-Saxon origins. The slaves, being nothing more than chattel, were taught to emulate their masters. To do otherwise would result in punishment or in the worst instance, loss of life.

Such actions were deemed necessary by the planters to placate and subjugate a people against whom an enormous atrocity had been enacted. These ignorant planters believed that the construction of these false social standards could act as a panacea to the wounded psyche of the slave population.

Generation after generation handed over this style of hypocritical living to their offspring. After a while the planters had no need to enforce such draconian counter-cultural behavior. It had become ingrained into the ways and means of the slaves and their descendants. Over a period of time an unwritten constitution was enshrined into black Barbadian culture. This bore no resemblance to the natural and ethnic origins of the Barbadian. It was borrowed, and indeed the garments that came with such lifestyle resembled some that could very well be found in jolly old England.

Any person or persons who failed to toe such colonial and royalist lines were immediately labeled as unconventional and radical. It is for this reason that the planters had established the Royal Barbados Police Force and had constructed Her Majesty's Prison at Glendairy. It is important for any historian worth his salt to be cognizant of this fact. Any denial of such may result in the wanna-be historian taking a new label—the Twistorian.

These two institutions were and still are for the sole purpose of protecting the non-blacks, incarcerating the blacks who step out of line, serving the interests of the planter hegemony class, and reassuring them that all is well and that things are under control and so they could keep on subjugating these hapless souls and making profit from the sweat of their labour.

As time progressed the dissidents were turning out younger and younger recruits. After the 1937 riots and the Moyne Commission had been handed in, the fact of life was that business as usual continued on the island. The same discriminatory practices, the same inhumane conditions and same psychological bullying still obtained as was the case prior to the riots.

In the poor, depressed areas, poverty was making its presence felt with the emergence of street children whose only crime was that they refused to die of starvation and boredom in a conservative Barbados that had little or no regard for them or their parents.

These children took to the streets, for they scarcely had any kind of a structure that could be called home, and the resulting mischief had become embarrassing to the nobility of the island. Therefore, a second form of correctional institution had to be set up—hence Dodd's for the boys, and Summervale for any female deviants.

These street children, like children the world over, needed some form of engagement to help spend their time. Having no money to source any toys from the department stores of the day, these youngsters called upon their ingenuity and inventive nature. Using any materials that came immediately to hand and were discarded by the rich folks as garbage, they devised vehicles and implements for their own amusement.

Society, in order to place a line of demarcation between the rulers and the unruly, made it necessary to define these young ones by the price and design of their toys. I once heard a middle class bigot refer to his standard of life in this way "You separate the men from the boys by the size and the price of their toys."

In much the same way, the price (or lack thereof) of the children's toys was used as a line of separation.

The richer kids had a toy motor car propelled by pedals which could seat at least two persons. These could be purchased from Cave Shepherd, Fogarty's or Woolworth department stores. The poor kids dismantled fruit crates and searched the garbage dumps around mechanical and engineering workshops for discarded ball bearings to use as wheels. They then utilized cord to act as steering, risking the ire of both motorist and patrolling lawmen by speeding down some steep incline that had a sharp bend at the end of it in order to showcase their handling of speed and navigation of the craft.

Needless to say some accidents occurred, and many a youngster had his head crushed beneath the wheels of an unsuspecting motorist.

This was a perfect excuse for the lawmen to decree these makeshift vehicles outlawed. Cumbersome as they were, when pursued by the lawmen, the youngsters would have to evacuate the trolley and jump any nearby walls or galvanized fences to escape apprehension. This would initiate the youngster's first foray into the world of fugitives. They were called the 'wild boys'.

Most 'wild boys' usually played truant from school in order to dive for coins in the shipping's and on some occasions in the wharf. They lived a carefree life and didn't care if Sunday came on a Monday, or if Christmas fell on a Good Friday. Ostracized by society, it was a crime to even befriend any of these at the time. Arming themselves with the Bajan version of the catapult—an implement made from the Y-section of guava trees and reinforced with rubber strands—the guttaperk was an instant ticket to the Government Industrial School at Dodds for anyone caught with one.

The wild boys didn't give two hoots, and defied the lawmen every chance they got. They were swift of foot and agile in movement and to boot very good swimmers and divers. They existed on their psychical attributes, since being non-compliant with the school system, cranial fortitude was a luxury they could ill afford.

The scooter took the place of the bicycle, as one of these was too expensive for the poverty-stricken parents of these wild boys. The scooter was made of wood and metal, and had ball bearings as wheels. Now it is here that the ingenuity of the individual came into play. Any lack thereof could ultimately result in the lawmen making an easy apprehension.

The scooter was divided into two sections by an implement called the shaft. One section, the place where you place your feet, carried the only means of slowing or stopping the vehicle. This was done by placing your heel on the rear bearing. The other section was used by the hands for steering. The shaft connected the hand section to the foot section of the scooter.

When one was being chased by the lawmen the rider

would pull the shaft and thus separate the vehicle into two sections. These were tossed into some nearby bushes and the escape would be exacted on foot. If the scooter was found by the lawmen, in their anger it was broken into pieces.

The roller was a simpler form of vehicle, so to speak. It consisted of an old bicycle rim which was made of steel with a piece of iron bent and shaped to act as steer. When the roller was set in motion it depended greatly on the fleet-footedness of its jockey as well as the softness of his hands to navigate.

Groups of wild boys got together and held races with these rollers. These races were called Derbys. The resulting noise that was made when steel, iron and asphalt collided was resounding, and some deemed it a public nuisance to the ears. Needless to say this went a long way in nominating the wild boys as Public Enemy Number One by the general populace, who could be easily distracted by the slightest of events given the socio–economic problems which kept them under perpetual stress.

Therefore, little or no sympathy was given to the seemingly delinquent youths who had nothing better to do but run around the streets making loud and ear-screeching noises.

The existence of a wild boy was a crude one at best. Demonized by lawmen, ostracized by their peers and marginalized by the general public, they lived a life that followed many to their graves, and when remembered their titles would be unceremoniously attached "Oh, he was a wild boy."

Observation of such bigotry and division made me acutely aware of the country I was living in. What has amazed me over the years is how ignorant the Barbadian is of his own country and his belief in the false pretence that Barbados might be the freest black nation on earth. On the contrary, I have found that the freedom of which Bajans so openly boast is oftentimes diluted with a bucket of disrespect for each other. Many a Barbadian can be heard to remark that "I don't pay taxes for my mouth..." or "Nobody can't do me anything for talking out my mouth." These statements are ready-made licenses for the average Barbadian to assassinate each other's character, and to verbally assault the soft and timid to the extent that the bubble bursts and then all hell breaks loose.

Over the years I've come to see this island's people as similar to Israelites in the land of Egypt where even your brother can be your worst enemy in a dog-eat-dog, uncivil and uncouth society that boasts of God being one of their own, solely on the precept that every square inch of their landscape is dotted with churches, police stations and rum shops.

A hypocritical society such as this would most definitely have many social deviants lurking in the shadows, like so many Dr. Jekyll's and Mister Hyde's. In these modern times the wild boys look pale and harmless in comparison to today's gun-slinging, drug-trafficking thugs and gangsters.

Even now the implements and the vehicles that the wild boys had invented and had subsequently been ostracized for, have been given historical heritage status, and some now are being commercially distributed, as in the case of the scooter.

Many a wild boy of the past must be turning in their graves in silent protest to such developments.

The Wedding

Rixie was a boxer. At least that's I was told. When I knew Rixie he was a shopkeeper.

Rixie used to run a bar at the corner of Wellington and Nelson Streets in Bridgetown. Rixie's shop had the first juke box where for 25 cents you could select a song and watch the artist perform and listen as well. I remember hearing the late great Jackie Opel singing *Lonely Teardrops* in front of the same juke box, as thrilling and entertaining performance as any that could be enjoyed for a measly shilling.

Legend has it that Rixie was a fearsome fighter back in the day, who went by the *nomme de guerre* 'The Iron Tiger'. It was said that he was deadly in a clinch, and many an unsuspecting opponent suffered a series of below-the-belt punches unknown to the unsighted referee.

The Iron Tiger became a pussy-cat the day he clinched with Christine.

The corner of Wellington and Nelson Streets. The building on the left is the former site of Rixie's Bar

Christine was a prostitute from Trinidad. And what made matters worse, Christine was extremely beautiful. She had the kind of face that seemed to kiss the morning sun and a complexion the color of cocoa butter. Her eyes shone like diamonds in her lovely face and when she applied make-up she resembled the legendary movie star Elizabeth Taylor. They both possessed the same roundness of features and that wild-eyed innocence that never betrayed the devil woman lurking inside.

It was this beauty that brought Rixie to a sudden demise. The Iron Tiger fell hook, line and sinker the first day he laid eyes on Christine as she paraded down Nelson Street, dressed in hot pants cutting close to the crevices in a style that only Trinis can employ with halter top to match displaying her soft, luscious cocoa skin, a pair of suede knee-length boots, and an attitude made to provoke lust and carnal intention for the specific purpose of acquiring legal tender of any amount, the price exacted for services rendered. Such an attitude left grown men drooling into their beverages as she sauntered jauntily along the seedy streets of Bridgetown. Nelson Street was on fire.

Rixie fell for the trap and immediately entrusted his business, his heart, his soul, his mind and indeed his entire being to this Trinidadian bombshell of a woman, all in exchange for a few stolen moments beneath the covers of his bed.

Christine, on the other hand, having found a sugar-daddy faster than she expected, decided to play the field with every young available Bajan stud she could wrap her gorgeous Trinidadian legs around. Rixie was by now enamoured, and couldn't see the forest for the trees, just as long as Christine returned to his humble domicile after enjoying her many romantic trysts. Bajan society soon made an issue of Christine's infidelities, viewing them as improper compensation for Rixie's never-ending benevolence.

In no time Rixie countered reason by proposing marriage to Christine, who readily accepted. This meant a one-way ticket to Barbadian citizenship, as the island had just become independent from Britain and had included a 'nationality by marriage to a Barbadian' clause in its new constitution. Now she had everything she had hoped to achieve in no time spent. All that was left to be done was to organize an event-of-the-year marriage, one that would be on the lips of everyone for decades to come.

The wedding itself was a farce. I remember the sordid affair. The ceremony was conducted on a Saturday evening at St. Ambrose church. Being a member of the church choir, I had a front row seat to view the entire proceedings.

Rixie and Christine, both people of ill repute who resided in Barbados' only red light district, Nelson Street, probably sent invitations to every prostitute, lesbian, homosexual, convict, alcoholic, addict, criminal and bandit in the Southern Caribbean.

On the evening in question the environs of St. Ambrose Church resembled a fish market. With the colorful language and raucous behavior, a person bereft of sight could quite easily have believed themselves to be on the compound of the Bay Street fish market instead of the Holy premises of a place of worship, such was the ruction and din of this conspicuous affair.

The dress code of the day was inevitably XXX-rated. Skin was in. Exposed thighs and climbing hemlines complimented bulging cleavages, and the sheerness of clinging materials amongst the females left many eyes popping out of their heads, for it seemed like the women had made a concerted effort to parade themselves as scantily attired as possible.

But the men, on the other hand, came out looking resplendent and in sartorial elegance. They left nothing to be desired. Every-day drunkards and perennial low-lifes, scumbags and pick-pockets, all lent to the occasion, if not for a moment, the solemnity it demanded—a case of classic 'haute couture'. And so the opinion of many of the by-standers was that the men in general had saved the day and made the event less of a side-show than it was beginning to resemble.

And then there was the arrival of the loquacious 'Black Trousers'.

Black trousers

Deep inside the seedy back streets and alleys of Eastern Bridgetown lies the underbelly of Bajan life and its harsh realities, a world virtually non-existent to the average conservative-minded Barbadian. Here can be found a proliferation of watering holes commonly referred to as 'rum shops'.

The rum shop can be sometimes tarred and feathered (by the teetotalers none the least), albeit for the wrong reasons. Then again, the alcohol consumer will have his day in court by glorifying his neighborhood dispensary as a place of absolute necessity. Whatever the case, there remains one residual fact about the rum shop—it is a grassroots university where the hard knocks of life are presided over by its many philosophers and teachers.

Any small country with a large population concentrated in tiny villages and hamlets, especially one with a steamy tropical climate, needs some institution where the inhabitants can socialize away from the confines of the daily drudgery in order to unwind, relax, entertain and be entertained, argue, play, eat and drink.

In a country such as Barbados where the majority of the landscape is cultivated under sugar cane and where, as legend has it, the first rum was made under the facetious title of 'rumbullion', there is no mystery as to why alcohol is the main substance consumed and abused by the populace.

Young and old; blacks and whites; the rich, poor, religious, atheist, high-class, middle-class; and those of the lower socio-economic bracket all enjoy a good grog at some time or as in the case of those who prefer extremities to normalcy, all the time. In Barbadian culture the rum shop has stamped its authority and engraved its multi-usefulness into Bajan mainstream, so much so that in modern times it has become a heritage tourist attraction.

Growing up as a lad in the middle sixties in pre-independence Barbados, the rum shop had a somewhat unwarranted stigma attached to it, whereby no so-called decent person would be caught dead inside or near one of these dens of iniquity. Only the unholy and those in need of penitence would be bold enough to visit therein. Funny how times have changed. Now the valued and highly protected tourists are encouraged to visit the Rum Shop and enjoy a real slice of Barbadian lifestyle.

The rum shop is forbidden territory to small children

because of the colorful language within the ear shot of all and sundry on a daily and nightly basis, and the occasional spats of violence likely to occur when many a rum drinker reached fever pitch and became reckless and ignorant.

In the case where some rum shops doubled as a grocery and drug store, a line of demarcation was installed so that teetotalers and minors did not hitherto come into contact with the rum drinkers as they went about their separate transactions.

There existed and still exists those who had the habit, but not the financial wherewithal, to maintain such habits. These are locally referred to as the rum pimps (not to be confused with those who pander and caretake ladies of the night in the United States of America). The term 'pimp' is used loosely here to denote a person who lives by auxiliary means to satisfy his foolhardy ideas.

These usually spend their entire lives in the pursuit of the ultimate illusion of the intoxicant high and permeate the proximity of the rum shop without regard for personal hygiene, healthy nutrition, or performance of substantial duty to enhance their general self-improvement, drinking gallons of rum each month, and as in the words of the famous folk song, oblivious to the world and their rancor.

> *When ah got in muh liquor*
> *Don't talk to me*
> *When ah drink mih rum*

Don't talk to me
De beers in mih head
And de rum in mih knee
When ah got in mih liquor
don't talk to me

Nowadays local soca artist Gorg has re-immortalized the whole scenario with his spin of a different kind.

Meh woman left me
she gone and left me
she really horn me
she really horn me
Woao wo oo
but I got my rum!

These addicts come in both genders and all ages. Unlike marijuana and cocaine, this drug is not only legal, but of virtual importance to the Gross Domestic Product of an import-based country. Rum is one of the foremost exports Barbados has to offer, much in the same way as cocaine is to Columbia, and therefore any social disease it spreads is handled as quietly and secretively as possible. For example, a family which has a chronic alcoholic in their midst will have much more sympathy for that individual than for one with a cocaine or marijuana habit, who would be in no uncertain terms written off as worthless. The alcoholic would first be defined by his better qualities, with the added footnote that "He likes lil' grog in between, nothing wrong with dat."

It is against this background that I introduce to you Black Trousers.

Black Trousers was a woman. To say that Black Trousers was an alcoholic would be to state the obvious in mild terms. She was of dark pigment and had skin like leather. She was for the most part unkempt, probably in her sixties. When I knew her, Black Trousers lived for a shot of rum and the burning sensation it provided.

One thing that was plain to see about her was that life had kicked her in the teeth so many times before that her game was now at an all-time low. But that didn't stop her from being an affront to all and sundry, with little or no respect or regard for anyone, especially when in the miserable clutches of cold turkey. It was at such times that she employed a reverse psychology as a form of revenge to make herself feel of worth as a human being.

Black Trousers would not refrain from blistering any unsuspecting person with verbal abuse if refused the pittance she begged for, and spent many a night in the lock-up at the Bridge Harbor Police Station for using indecent language. As a matter of fact, along with indecent exposure, that was the only misdemeanor she really ever committed. Such behavior prompted many a magistrate to sentence her to a couple of days at Glendairy Prisons when the courts thought that she either needed to be taught a lesson or given some time to cool off or in the disgraceful extreme, she had overstepped the bounds of impropriety.

In those days of colonial and Royal British control over the island, whenever royalty was in town, the authorities found it important to skid-row her for the duration of the visit to avoid the potentially dangerous occurrence of her making a fool of not only herself (for Black Trousers had gained a PhD. in that venture), but the good name of the country before the visiting dignitary.

Needless to say this would be to the chagrin of the custodian on duty at the Main Guard at the time. He would invariably have to put up with her rantings and ravings for the night, not to mention her incessant cravings for the fire water and subsequent abuse about his mother and the private regions of her anatomy when refused such.

Now at Rixie's wedding, already made into a community circus sideshow by the various notorious and nefarious characters invited, all that was needed for the show-stopper was the arrival of Black Trousers in all her drunken glory.

The village Harbor Policeman, Tom Paine, stood at the ready to interrupt and remove any likely disturbance inside and around the solemn and sanctimonious precincts of St. Ambrose Church.

Already the buzz inside the church was growing into a noisy din with each passing second as the crowd awaited the arrival of the bride. Rixie stood waiting for his spouse, dressed in splendor for his big moment in time. Indeed he looked the part of 'Man of the Moment'.

His recently tailored red suit sat upon his slender frame like that of a statesman or politician. A small bouquet of flowers adorned his top left breast pocket. A lily-white shirt accessorised by a tie of the same color as the suit itself, and a pair of cuff links of gold and black peeped from beneath his jacket sleeves. A pair of snakeskin shoes brought in by one of his seamen friends rounded off this matrimonial ensemble, much to the admiration of the many ladies of the night and mamasongs in the congregation. As was mentioned before, everybody who was anybody in the world of prostitution and Bajan under-life was present at this 'glorious' occasion.

"Gaw-bline-yuh, yuh cock rat!" Black Trousers. "Yuh waiting in vain!"

The entire congregation turned to locate the general position of this familiar, raspy and rum-soaked voice.

"Can't trust me a shot o' rum, but gone and married a Trinidadian whore."

The church erupted like a Friday night at the movies. The priest was livid. The choristers, feigning mocked indifference but knowing all too well the significance of Black Trousers' words, started to snicker in silence.

"She gone back to Trinidad wid all yuh money, yuh cock dice."

Rixie was becoming noticeably impatient and started fidgeting with his tie. Candy Kidd, the best man and another alcoholic—but today a picture of sobriety—was whispering words of encouragement to him.

The priest asked for quiet in as stern a voice as he could muster, and the din descended from its crescendo to the allowed hushed murmurs associated with people who found it hard to remain completely silent for extended periods of time. Black Trousers continued the sledging.

"She tek yuh money and gone Tunupuna." Black Trousers said, plagiarizing the words to that famous Merrymen song *Millie Gone To Brazil*.

The church erupted again. This time even Rixie found it hard to suppress a somewhat timid smile. By now the vicar was blowing his top.

"This is the house of the Lord and will be treated as such," he said. "Any further outburst of the sort and I will order this ceremony over."

The local bad-johns started grumbling under their breaths. No doubt their minds were on the abundance of food and drink that awaited at the reception house.

Black Trousers was by now engaging in a game of hide and seek with Tom Paine. Ably assisted by a mischievous crowd outside the church, she weaved and meandered her way between them and moved from window to window to proclaim her exhortations. Tom Paine was having the time of his life trying to track her down from the confines of his bicycle.

"A whore and a thief mek God laugh!"

This time the congregation suppressed their mirth into smoldering sniggers, and the priest continued his meditations in the sure knowledge that his words had taken the desired effect.

Millions Think So!

Christopher Randolph 'Rannie' Hoyte used to run a rum shop at the corner of Queens' and Beckwith Streets. He was an eccentric, but he was eccentric in his own peculiar way. Rannie had his own style of eccentricity which came fully loaded with its own mannerisms, its own philosophy and a wide assortment of erstwhile witty sayings, some of which were traditional and the rest were homemade concoctions designed to hit home the desired message on impact.

Rannie used to be an omnibus conductor some years earlier, and had salted away some of the takings he had acquired during his underhand dealings with the bus company. Being a country bumpkin, he headed for the bright lights of the city. There he met a woman who was in her senior years and desperately in need of some intimate liaison, which Rannie readily provided.

The woman had a shop that had fallen on hard times and Rannie's venture capital had been more

Building at the corner of Queen and Bechwith Streets which once housed Rannie's Bar

than welcome in the circumstances. But then the unforeseen occurred. The woman died suddenly, leaving Rannie as the sole beneficiary and proprietor of the establishment.

The nearby residents were his first customers and the shop at the time sold mainly soda pop and biscuits. Meanwhile Rannie cut 'short pool' from the thriving bingo and poker games that were carried on at the back of the shop.

Eventually, Rannie raised enough money to provide a substantial amount of stock and was off and running like a day at the races. He always trumpeted that his first customers, whom he considered to be the mainstay of his business, would always be close to his heart and no one could come between them. These customers just happened to be the neighborhood corner boy who spent their time gambling and consuming Rannie specials.

In those days a soda pop was sold for eighteen

cents, and one biscuit went for the price of one cent. Therefore for the price of twenty-five cents one could purchase the quite handy snack of soda pop and biscuits, while attempting to break the poker game.

However, special or no special, Rannie soon reneged on his promise when the ranks of his customers were swollen to include the likes of Johnnie Salt Bags, who was a police sergeant, Austin Boots, a merchant from the Brittons Hill area, and other men of great means who were consistent consumers of the 'big mouth drinks' that Rannie had now placed on display.

So the specials and their consumers had to take their place when the 'big mouth drinkers' were in town. As a matter of fact, Rannie preferred that they were not seen at all, and would pontificate this somewhat subtly by refusing to sell soda pop and biscuits when his lordly friends were around.

As time went by, Rannie hit a slump when his 'big mouth drinking' friends found some other watering hole to patronize. Now Rannie had to resort to the stone he once refused. The specialists forgave him, but never let him forget. All Rannie could submit to the youngsters was "I, the accused."

As the years rolled along Rannie's business became more prosperous. Some of the specialists had graduated to the lucrative work as seamen that now became the order of the day for any able-bodied young man at the time. Returning home after sometimes spending more than six months at sea and being paid off with twenty or thirty thousand pounds sterling, in the days when one pound equaled four Barbados dollars and eighty cents, these young men suddenly found themselves with more disposable income than they could handle. The glamour girls of the day volunteered to cream the excess and trim their sails. Indeed some of these girls had the capacity to completely knock the wind out of their sails.

However, these seamen always remembered their humble beginnings and never patronized any other shop but Rannie's. Pretty soon the corner became a hive of activity whenever the seamen were in town. Non-stop partying and drinking were the order of the day and everyone had that glow of expectancy as each day some new person would be inducted into the world of those who went down to sea in ships and did business in great waters.

The ladies of the day, as opposed to the ladies of the night, kept their men in close tow and never left their side. To do so could be to their detriment, as these guys were the most sought after on the island at the time.

Having a man who spent three months on the rock gave these women all the room they needed to play the field when their men were out to sea. Meanwhile they kept up the pretence of being faithful to their unsuspecting spouses. Add to this the luxury of receiving the latest clothing and jewels, not to mention large sums of money, in those days known as allotment money.

These were the late sixties and early seventies, the years when the British Harrison Line and the American Star Line, along with the Booth line and numerous other shipping lines, were recruiting Barbadian males to work on their vessels. All those school leavers who had failed the Common Entrance exam, and who had subsequently attached their names to list of persons desirous of joining the ranks of seamanship, suddenly were now transporting big ships to all parts of the globe and were navigating and catering in such faraway places as Africa, Australia, the cold waters of Europe, as well as the Pacific and Atlantic Oceans.

Just imagine this: a young boy who had just a few short months ago been deemed non-academic and useless, was now directing great ships through such diverse places as the River Thames, the Suez Canal and the Panama Canal.

Compensation for such labors was bountiful and the seamen now had an opportunity to make a life for themselves much faster than their more academic mates with all their education and promise of well-paying jobs.

Sad to relate, not many of them ever really fulfilled their true financial potential. Distracted by the three W's—no, not Worrell, Weekes and Walcott but wine, women and worthlessness—they lavished away millions of dollars among them. Rannie was one of the beneficiaries, but try as he might he too was unable to resist the urge to splurge and this led to one of his famous philosophies "Boy, immoral earnings don't last."

George Puny

Rannie had many customers, some of whom paid a visit to the shop on a daily basis. It was around such persons that the theatre of the establishment revolved. Some more than others made it worthwhile for Rannie to keep his doors opened for extended periods during the night. At such times Rannie would enlist the services of a trusted few souls to continue for him while he took a much needed nap.

Due to the lack of proper inventory on Rannie's part, profits were untold and many of the trusted souls would pocket substantial sums of money in his absence. Rannie never quarreled about such behavior and would proceed to restock the shop, albeit on a commission basis.

It was a virtual free for all and everyone got in line to assist Rannie and ultimately help themselves to some of these profits. This continued for some time until one day Rannie was unable to meet his commitment with the travelling salesman who distributed the liquor to him. Such an embarrassing situation this proved to be that the seamen were called upon to hastily pool together some funds in order to stall the foreclosure of the shop. The seamen had saved the day for Rannie and the hangers-on.

George Puny was a regular at the shop. He came every day around the same time. One could say that when it came to Rannie, George was punctual. Every day just before noon he would arrive, and for the next two hours or so would entertain as well as inform the youngsters who limed outside the shop, playing games such as warri, checkers and dominoes.

George was of dark complexion. In fact, he looked as if he would turn blue at any moment, especially when he ventured out of the midday sun. He was about five feet three and of slim build. He had a habit of wearing way too many clothes than was needed in a country such as Barbados. Usually George would be wearing two to three shirts sometimes accompanied by a woolen turtle necked sweater, about three pants and four pairs of socks which he gathered over his pants bottoms. This exaggerated fashion ensemble would be topped off with a sturdy pair of boots made of leather.

Oftentimes George spoke with an American accent. When he became enraged, he would smoothly revert to a strong Bajan accent, fully embellished with the local expletives.

During his visit to Rannie's Bar, George would partake of copious amounts of straight rum shots chased with some water. He would invariably offer one to Rannie, and they would raise their glasses in tandem in a spontaneous toast to any relevant of the issues of the day. Then with a loud "Aaaaaaah!" they would each in turn chase from the bottle of cold water and wipe their mouths as if they had just finished consuming some delectable piece of culinary delight. Their eyes would turn red, reminiscent of Count Dracula in one of his murderous moments, and their faces would contort beyond recognition as the deadly fire water cascaded down their palates and into the labyrinths of their stomachs.

"So how the hell are yuh doing, Rannie muh man?" George would say this in the best New York accent he could muster, after regaining his composure from the assault he had performed on his sobriety a few short seconds earlier.

Rannie would answer the same way every time, no matter what his position or disposition was.

"Oh George! I'm not as good as the fellow who is better than me, but I am definitely better than the one who is worse off than me." Rannie would eventually surmise, much to George's amusement.

"That's my man Rannie. Never one to complain." George would reply, sounding more like John Wayne the legendary cowboy and movie star.

"Yuh know George," Rannie would continue. "It's what we put into life that we ultimately get out of it." Rannie spoke in clear grammatical tones. He did this from time to time, especially when dishing out any of his philosophical offerings.

"Millions come into a world and never contribute anything of substance, and when they are about to leave they want the biggest of funerals complete with eulogy and wake and such like, yuh know?"

George would shake his head and agree with Rannie as he propped himself against the counter in a snazzy gangster lean. George had all the styles of a New Yorker even if he didn't dress the part, for his clothes were all of a far earlier vintage, and looked as if they were sourced from the Salvation Army which was situated near to George's domicile. Nary a soul would venture to mention this to Ol' George, that is, if you were not afraid of running the risk of being on the receiving end of a vicious tongue whipping. For George, despite all his American twang, could wield a proper round of cussing if driven to the point where he thought that nothing else would prevail.

George gave boast of being a boxer. Indeed George gave boast of being many things, especially when he was tipsy and on the verge of getting plastered. For between Rannie and himself, one couldn't surmise who became drunk the easiest. Rannie would as a course of habit become intoxicated at least twice every day. Early in the morning he would rise and open his establishment, then he would entertain his early customers and knock back a few as a mark of appreciation. By the early hour of ten o'clock Rannie would start showing signs of an early TKO. His speech would start to slur and his manner become somewhat agitated. Then George Puny would arrive and he would be all over the bar shouting for Rannie.

As I said, George boasted of being a pugilist of some sort. He also boasted of being a cook in the Gestapo prisons of Hitler's Germany, while serving time as a prisoner of war, during the Second World War.

"I cooked for the Army and the Navy in Germany, yuh fucking cunt, and poisoned the whole fucking set ah dem."

This time George punctuated his American accent with his normal sprinkling of Bajan expletives.

"I even cook for Rasputin, Houdini and the Devil, and all three suffered the same fate."

The young boys would howl with laughter and the atmosphere was charged in anticipation of more fireworks from George.

Nothing could touch George's graphic descriptions of any of his many pugilistic battles as a fighter in the United States. For all intents George was what was known in fight circles as a step-ladder boxer—one who was used by better fighters to compromise their fight record and add some flourish to their career ratings. George claimed he was paid handsomely to take the occasional fall, or dive in some instances. Probably with a small compensation of whisky along with some cash, as that was all that George would really need in the first place.

One such description I can clearly remember, word for word.

"There was this guy from somewhere in Philadelphia; a white guy," George said, his head lifted to the sky as if in search of some apparition from the heavens. "He was about twenty pounds heavier than me, but that didn't bother me; what I lacked in weight I made up for with style."

George dropped into a fighter's crouch in much the same way as Smoking Joe Frazier. Come to think of it now, George did have some similarities that reminded one of the former heavyweight champion. Placing his hands to his face as a guard in the classic fighting stance, he bobbed and weaved like a piece of cork on a rough sea.

"He was a southpaw, yuh know, one of those who lead with their left hand. Quite unorthodox really."

George was now beginning to sound like Walter Cronkite on fight night.

"He had this funny way of dropping his right hand to his waist every time he was about to throw a left jab."

By now the shop would be crowded to the brim, as the young boys gathered around to hear this graphic blow by blow account.

"So I thought that this was due to some technical deficiency on his part, and so I set out to capitalize on this blatant misuse of technique."

The noise we made could raise the dead in Westbury

cemetery about two miles away.

"We went into a clinch and he pushed me off like a bag of feathers; and then I saw it coming. He set up to jab and took position, his right hand dropping to his waist. I shifted my weight from one foot to the next. Then I wound up to break this man's jaw."

George paused to toss back a shot of rum that Rannie had supplied compliments of the house in order to spruce up George's delivery of the story.

"Yeah man, as I was saying, I wound up like a cork screw and telegraph a left hook of my own. And then..." George paused again.

The young boys waited with bated breath to hear the outcome of this most interesting encounter.

"So wha' happen George? You knock he out?" Someone asked. Another pause punctuated the air. Then he continued.

"Be-Jesus-Christ, the next thing I know, I feel somebody slapping me in my face." By now George had slipped back into pure Bajan dialect. "And I smell somebody pushing smelling salts underneath my nose."

The young boys bawled and fell to the floor laughing raucously.

"I hear a man telling me..." This time George slipped back into a southern drawl. "*George, George! You okay man?*" This was my trainer. A fucking thief if there was ever one. '*Ya had me scared there for a moment.*' What happened? I kinda lost it there for a while. '*Man*

George you walked into a thunderous uppercut. Never saw it coming. Hit ya like a ton a bricks. Ref could have counted to a hundred, it won't a mattered, and George you went out like the lights at Rikers Island late at night.' Boy I felt something the size of a cricket ball on top of my eye and try as I might I couldn't seem to get the damn thing to open." George said with a glazed look in his eyes.

"Oldest trick in the book, George, the bastard set you up man'. What the fuck. You know what ah mean? You win some and you lose some." George said eloquently, pretending to sound gracious in defeat, but feeling more like a dead duck in a dry pond.

With that Rannie placed another shot of rum on the counter and George disposed of it in the accustomed manner.

Haddock

Carl St. Aubun Haddock was even more eccentric than Rannie. Haddock was a royalist, loyalist monarchist. He believed in the monarchial system and was loyal to the Royal Family, and Great Britain.

He even dressed the part on occasions. Like on the day of the opening of Parliament, or the presentation of the Annual Budget Speech, Carl would be looking all so resplendent in his top hat and tails much in the likeness of an English Statesman. Nonetheless on closer inspection, you would see that his garments, even though sartorial in appearance, were worse for wear in actual condition and badly in need of laundering.

This didn't stop Haddock from mingling amongst the intelligentsia of the day, and his arrival was met with much fanfare, reminiscent of that associated with the Governor. More often than not it was mainly in jest as the crowd guffawed at this wannabe aristocrat. Haddock, in his conceit, would mistakenly think this to indicate his revered subjects showing their affection and adulation.

Haddock's burning lifelong ambition was to acquire a seat in the House of Assembly as an independent candidate. He had no choice but to run as an independent, for no political party worth the paper its manifesto was written on would ever contemplate placing Haddock amongst their team of candidates. He was that hopeless as a politician.

Haddock had contested about five elections and in total had aggregated no more than twenty-five votes. He once ran against Ernest Deighton Mottley for the city seat. This was in the days of 'Free Food for You and Your Family' soup kitchens and 'Mottley Khaki' for school children. These ventures were all pet projects of the mayor of Bridgetown, Mr. Ernest Deighton Mottley, a colossus of a man in stature and one with massive political clout. It was a case of an ant versus an elephant.

One night during his campaign, Haddock asked his brother Rupert to say a few words on his behalf as a testimony. Rupert was a city character and somewhat of an eccentric himself. He had a speech impediment and walked with an ungainly gait due to a distended double hernia, known otherwise in Barbadian parlance as 'goadies'.

Rumor had it that a prominent police inspector who on occasion had used Rupert as a 'gopher', had given him a sizeable sum of money to take to his wife who was waiting at home. Rupert, cognizant of the fact that the inspector's wife in question had a promiscuous love of money and was prone to infidelities, decided to concoct a ruse of his own. He proceeded to pretend that he was offering the woman the money as payment for her sexual favors. Rupert had promised the woman that their affair, sordid as it was, would be a total secret. Convinced of this, the woman capitulated and allowed Rupert to defile her matrimonial bed and take full advantage of her infidelities. When the inspector arrived home that day he inquired of his wife if she had received the money that he had sent. All the duped woman could do was to swallow her pride and answer in the affirmative.

Rupert hobbled onto the platform that night and stood before the lectern. Haddock adjusted the microphone to suit Rupert's height and the small crowd waited anxiously to hear this tongue-tied leprechaun deliver.

"Good night ladies and gentlemen."

Rupert surprised everyone with his verbal clarity and microphone etiquette.

"People all, I is Carol bruddah."

Because of his speech impediment, Rupert was prone to referring to this brother as 'Carol' instead of Carl.

"But he ain't no pucking good, don't vote fuh he, vote fuh Mottley. He does gi' me clothes. Carol doan gi' nuh body nutten."

The crowd roared its approval. They only saw Haddock as comic relief to the whole affair of elective politics and nothing more.

Haddock was seething with rage, and to show his disgust he spat near the feet of his brother. He then proceeded to reposition the diaphragm of the microphone away from Rupert's mouth in an effort to abort this assassination of his character.

Rupert continued his harangue outside the frequency of the public address system, and could vaguely be heard berating his poor brother.

"Carol is just an impostor, he ain't no pucking good."

Haddock signaled to his security to remove Rupert and avoid further humiliation.

Rupert was known to be a stick-licker in his earlier years, and in these times he never ventured anywhere without his dearly beloved 'Daisy', a sturdy piece of guava tree limb, the sole purpose of which was to inflict pain and to maim and disfigure. Indeed it even accompanied him to church on the few occasions that he chose to trespass in the House of the Lord.

The security approached Rupert with trepidation and caution. Employing diplomacy, they finally managed to cajole him into leaving the platform and allowing the meeting to continue. Haddock regained his composure somewhat, and cleared his throat before he spoke.

"Let me apologize for my brother's behavior. You see he is in possession of less than four ounces of brain.

This is what occurs when you allow mendicants to speak on your behalf."

Haddock offered in a vain attempt to do some damage control, and pronouncing the word mendicants with specific emphasis on the last syllable of the word, thereby causing to sound as 'mendicunts'. It was like the Mobile Cinema featuring Bud Albert and Lou Costello.

On one other occasion Haddock ran against the DLP stalwart, who would later go on to become Prime Minister at Mr. Barrow's death. However, on this occasion Mr. Sandiford was running in the constituency of St. Michael South. Haddock held a meeting at Dunlop Lane, one of the areas inside the constituency. This was situated a stone's throw away from Culloden Farm, the official residence of the Prime Minister at the time.

Haddock began by thanking the small audience for braving the inclement weather to attend his meeting. It meant nothing to describe to him that everyone present was indeed from the same gap where the meeting was being held.

He continued by outlaying the problems that the country was facing, and then he went on to highlight—in his words—the many shortcomings of the government. After this vitriolic tirade against the oligarchy of the day, Haddock then outlined the way forward for these, as he put it, "hapless and disenfranchised members of the Barbadian proletariat."

His diatribe was progressing smoothly and the crowd was listening with rapt attention, if not complete interest. Haddock outdid himself, his oratorical skills coming to the fore. Applause after applause greeted every one of Haddocks prophetic exhortations.

Haddock turned up the heat in an attempt to hammer home his initiatives and construct some argument against the Democratic Labor Party. Then, taking into consideration the aforementioned location of his meeting, Haddock committed the unthinkable act of going after the father of Independence, literally in his own backyard.

"And when these political criminals, such as big bulling Barrow...." he started, but this was as far as he got, for seemingly out of nowhere missiles of all descriptions and sizes began to rain down on the platform, and Haddock and his few helpers had to scamper to safety in order to preserve life and limb. How dare he bad-mouth Mr. Barrow in front of his dear loving supporters, and expect to get away with it?

On yet another occasion Haddock had fancied his chances against another DLP political champion, this time taking on the might of none other than the late Richie Haynes, who would later be known as Sir Richard Haynes, in a by-election to elect a member to sit in the House of Assembly representing the constituency of St. Michael South Central, and this which included Haddock's household. Haddock this time felt confident that he could for the first time in his political career make a serious impression on the result of an election. There were twelve persons abiding in his house, all of whom were eligible to vote and had indicated to Haddock that their vote was his and his alone.

On the morning of the by-election, Haddock had volunteered to transport some of the voters to the polling booth. One such person was an old lady by the name of Niecey. Niecey was an octogenarian and had been quite fond of Haddock and his colonial deportment. Being of the old school, no one could occasion her to find fault with this gentleman who spoke the Queen's English with such eloquence and flourish, and whose garments were of, as far as her poor eyesight could fathom, such impeccable order. On the other hand, she had had a personal relationship with the doctor Richie Haynes. He was her personal doctor. Herein lay the foundation for the ensuing comedy of errors that was to take place.

On arrival at the polling booth, Haddock made a last-ditch appeal for Niecey to give him her support.

"Don't forget Niecey, do the right thing and support your humble servant," he pleaded, making sure that he did not overstep the boundaries of electoral impropriety by soliciting votes on the day of an election.

Niecey had replied earnestly in the affirmative, and Haddock breathed a sigh of relief, in the knowledge that he had procured another notch of support on his political gun.

With that Niecey made her way with the able assistance of Haddock to cast her vote. Haddock remained outside to further assist her into the waiting vehicle when her five minutes of democratic power had elapsed.

After a few short minutes Niecey returned from the booth and gave Haddock the 'thumbs up' sign. Haddock embraced her and thanked her profusely for doing the right thing.

"Carol, you never had to doubt me, I woulda never left you out, all two ah wunna belong to me," she told the by now shocked and stunned Haddock.

"I gi' you one and I gi Richie de other one," she told a by now livid Carl St. Auburn Haddock.

Haddock muttered under his breath to the old woman, "Jesus Christ Niecey, yuh gone and spoil de fucking vote."

On the night of the tabulations, the returning officer announced that Carl St. Aubun Haddock had mustered the large amount of twelve votes, and had thus included his own vote.

Haddock, sensing victory, immediately called for a recount. After all, with the twelve family members and their certain votes along with his own vote, and then add that to his recently garnered support due to his 'tenacity, and will power, which was second to none,' surely he must have put a sizeable dent in the returns of the other two candidates.

However, on the recount, it was discovered that quite a few votes had been spoiled. Indeed now the new improved count for Haddock stood at six votes. Haddock quickly recanted and once more made request, this time that the initial result be reinstated and that the returning officer completely forget his application for a recount. Later, during his 'thanksgiving speech', Haddock was heard to have said "There are a couple of blasted traitors in my family."

Rannie and Haddock locked horns almost every day and sometimes at night too. The routine was always the same. Rannie would ruffle the feathers of Haddock by replaying his many political skirmishes on the electoral front.

"Man Haddock, you think it is so..." Rannie would launch the attack on Haddock. "Whereas it is not so."

This would cause Haddock to scowl and look at Rannie with contemptible disdain.

"You never even saved your deposit. Man you ain't nothing but a miserable loser."

Rannie would continue to heap this abuse on Haddock. Haddock was keeping his cool under the circumstances.

"Do like me. Drink some rum and get drunk, try and forget about politics. Nobody eh go vote fuh you, we all know wha' it is you trying to get."

Rannie would pause for dramatic effect. When he felt he had made the desired impact on all those listening inside the shop, he would deliver the killer punch.

"Yeah man Haddock, the whole island knows you only using politics to get rich quick." Rannie was now speaking under the influence of the fire water he was consuming.

"If you would stop bulling, yuh would be better off." Haddock was prone to berate his attackers by casting aspersions on their sexual orientation, even though popular consensus had offered that he himself had engaged in similar sexual deviance in the past.

"Don't mind that." Rannie countered with some gusto. Everyone in the shop knew that Rannie was winding up to deliver a killer blow, possibly one way below the belt.

"Tell the shop how come big Rose had to done wid you. Talk man, leh de people hear."

Rannie was by now in top gear, and had the entire shop on his side. Haddock, sensing another loss, started to capitulate.

"If you know so much, you tell them nuh?"

Haddock had surrendered more in bluff than anything else. But Rannie was having none of it, and moved in for the kill.

"Tell them? Yuh want me to tell them? Awright then. She eh catch you with a next man in bed in de bake fowl?"

The patrons of the establishment laughed uncontrollably, some of them holding their sides and shaking with mirth.

This was dangerous ground that Rannie was trespassing on, for it was common knowledge that Haddock was a licensed gun holder, and carried a .38 calibre Smith and Wesson holstered under his left armpit at all times, in much the same way his brother never went anywhere without his trusted guava stick. Haddock carried his firearm on his person day and night.

Haddock broke into a smile and the whole thing simmered into an event of little or no importance. Such was the way of these men, who had a strange kind of respect for each other that only they themselves could understand. If one were of thin skin, or unable to accept verbal fatigue of any sort, this was not the place to be.

This wrangling would be a good starting point for those now venturing into the harsh world manhood. To the casual onlooker, it would appear that these guys were up in arms against each other. Nothing could be further from the truth, for in the case of emergency all hands would come on deck to rescue and provide assistance to anyone in the neighborhood who so desired. This network of community fellowship has been the main reason I've maintained a steady relationship with the folks of the Rebitts Land/Nelson Street areas.

Here I learnt how to make and keep friends for life. I have also been shown how one set of people can become known for things occurring in their domain over which they have no particular jurisdiction. I have seen as well, how these same actions can have catastrophic consequences on these same individuals, and how the ones responsible for these actions can walk away scott-free, with not even a slap on the wrist.

I have sat and listened with great trepidation as many Barbadian people have castigated the good people of the area for a dilemma which was no fault of their own. I have come to see this as unfair, and have spoken up against this every chance I got. I have been branded as a Nelson Street person, but this is a title that I carry with pride, for I have seen many other areas in this country which are decidedly more volatile than Nelson Street. I could name quite a few, but I will leave that for another discourse at a later date.

All in all, I must revert to the words of Christopher Randolph 'Hunt Dog' Hoyte "...millions think so, whereas, it is not so."

Part Three

Bay Primary

I was born on the seventeenth of June 1957. A Nigerian man and a Barbadian woman were my parents. I think I had to be born some time after midnight on the Monday. My mother probably thought she could have delivered me to the world on the Sunday (Corpus Christi) and so she prematurely named me Christopher. My other names were indicative of my genealogy. David was the name of my uncle, Adetokunbo Akinwale were the names my father had given me to remind me of my Nigerian background. Alleyne was my family name.

I was born in Paddington, London and my mother was a state registered nurse from Barbados who resided in the nurse's quarters at St. Mary's County Hospital. It is there I began my sojourn on this earth.

Right from the start I had been the center of attention for the ladies. While my mother made the rounds on the wards I would be placed in the care of any of the off-duty nurses.

London in the 1950s was, I came to realize, a melting pot of Caribbean cultures at the time. The wind rush had just deposited thousands of fortune seekers onto the British Isles. My mother was among them, my father having made the trek from the opposite side of the globe. The two, after a romantic tryst of some sort, copulated to allow my arrival into this world, just over a decade after the end of the Second World War. Right in time for me to take my place among the Baby Boomers.

The Beatles were running things on the scene of pop music and had just claimed that they were more popular than Jesus. The Teddy Boys had found out that there were some who were not intimidated by their flashy clothes, or their flashing switch blades. They were the ubiquitous Jamaicans. They carried an ounce to their bounce and didn't give two hoots about the Crown, the Throne, the Queen and anybody else in between. Even the way they walked was like a law unto their own selves; and to make matters worse, they loved a war and were even fonder of a riot.

I was born among all this social mayhem and even though I was in the pink of health, I was living inside a hospital. I had a Nigerian father who was threatening to abscond AWOL with me in tow back to Nigeria, already in the throes of the Biafran Massacre. Here one can see the predicament I was in at the tender age of four.

The Lord moves in mysterious ways, his wonders to perform. Through all the apprehension and anxiety my mother must have endured, up steps the Yorkshire Ripper to solve her problem.

My mother had meticulously taken care of an elderly white woman from the northern region of Yorkshire, and her family, in gratitude and appreciation had offered to take me with them to cold Yorkshire. They had reassured my mother that they would treat me as one of their own despite my obvious ethnic difference. My mother wasn't sure of this at first, but after their urgings she somehow relented and off to Yorkshire town I was taken.

As best as my memory serves, I can clearly state that Uncle Arthur and Auntie Mary lived up to their end of the bargain and I was never treated any different from the other young ones at the residence. If such had occurred, my mother, a no-nonsense person, would have removed me with immediate effect. In later years my mother had informed me that I seemed so happy in Yorkshire that I had almost forgotten her, and had to be told continuously that she was my mother.

The criminal element of the day put paid to any aspirations I might have had of becoming the first black child with caucasian parents. He was a murdering serial killer of the early sixties, and he had the devilish habit of cutting his victims' throats, leaving them just on the brink between life and death, after which this horrendous villain would tape record their gurgling pleas for help as they cascaded helplessly into the land of Nod. These recordings he would post to the local police in an attempt to show his ingenuity at modern day decimation. A couple of his victims were young boys around my age.

This was all the encouragement my mother needed to send to Barbados and announce to my grandmother that a little boy, her grandson, would be arriving ASAP. My mother arrived in Yorkshire with full intention of deporting me from the land of my birth in order to make sure that I would live to a ripe old age.

Thanks are in order, now that I look back on all this. I could so easily have fallen victim to the Yorkshire Ripper and never live to see the beauty of this island called Barbados.

And so, sometime in the year 1962, I was placed in the care of the captain of the British warship HMS Mountbatten, and after a rough ride across the Atlantic Ocean I arrived in Barbados via Antigua and Caracas. Minus any travelling documents and with nose running with snot from my first bout of bronchial asthma, an affliction that would haunt me up until the age of eighteen or nineteen.

On arrival at the newly constructed Bridgetown Deep Water Harbor, I can remember being perched on the shoulder of this white captain, my snotty nose depositing phlegm all over his tunic, and searching for the faces of my grandmother, my uncle and my adopted grandfather.

Earlier, back in England, my mother had shown me their photos and had commanded me to memorize these faces in order to readily identify them on my arrival. These photos were also given to the captain of the vessel, but I fear that he probably was in a fix, or so I have been told, due to the fact that every black person looks alike to white people much the same way that all persons of Mongolian extract appear to have the same likeness in features.

However, my roving eyes soon picked up my grandmother on the dock side. I promptly jumped from the captain's grasp and made my way down the gangway as quickly as I could, arriving safely in the arms of my grandmother with the captain, half-scared out of his wits, in hot pursuit.

This was my first performance on Barbadian soil, and believe me there were many more to come.

My journey from the Bridgetown Harbor to Henry's Lane took the route of Broad Street. Here I saw a Barbadian policeman for the first time. He was standing guard outside of Cave Shepherd across the street from what was then the Barclays Bank.

"Hey grandma, look, there's a bobby," I said loudly for all on the busy Broad Street to hear, in my Yorkshire/Cockney accent. This caused heads to immediately turn. This was 1962 and it was literally unheard of to hear a grown black man speaking with such an accent, furthermore a young boy of four years old. The colonialists of the time had succeeded in rearing up these souls so stupid under the Union Jack that they had thought that only the white man could speak in this way.

"Dah lil boy could speak too sweet," and then the prophecies started. "He is you family Miss Thing? He look like he gine be Prime Minister one ah dese days."

A short midget-like vendor told my grandmother. "He don't born bout here?" She further inquired.

"No." My grandmother answered. "He come from England my dear," Granny said while beaming with pride that I was the center of attention so early in the morning on one of Bridgetown's busiest streets.

"I see I gine have to clip you tongue," she joked with me, but at the time I could only guess the meaning of this new language I was being exposed to.

My education was started by a gentleman who taught at the school next to where I lived. It was called the Federal School and was owned by one DaCosta Edwards, who was a minister in the new Errol Barrow government.

My teacher, Mr. Small, came from St. Lucy. In those days a bus ride from St. Lucy to Bridgetown and back would have cost a small fortune, and to have to perform this task on a daily basis for five days would quickly erase any disposable income one could have acquired from a profession with such a measly emolument.

So Mr. Small was offered the use of the back room in our three bedroom chattel house in return for my tutelage. I had arrived during the start of the school term and had to wait for my chance to enter elementary school.

Small was so impressed with my standard of learning that he informed my grandmother that I was indeed ready to begin school in earnest.

I was sent to a private school on River Road called Miss Smith School. Here I encountered a living hell in the form of a female teacher whose sole intention was to make me right-handed at any cost, even if she had to amputate my left hand with her metal ruler. The teachers of the day had a quite silly belief that all left-handers owed the Devil a day's work. But to me this female teacher not only owed the devil a day's work, she was using me to pay him in full.

Nonetheless her sojourn on earth came to an abrupt end. I came to school one morning and was greeted with the announcement of her passing. I breathed a sigh of relief. Ever since then I have been a comfortable left-hander in the same vein as Sir Garfield Sobers and Brian Lara, etc.

Then there was John Gold. John Gold was white, the same age as myself, lived on River Road right in front of the school, and had a mother whom I assessed as being a racist. At least she didn't like me one bit. John Gold proceeded to attack me every chance he got, probably out of jealousy, for here was a black little boy from London town in 1960s semi-apartheid Barbados. Gold would have none of this, nor would his racist mother. She probably had instructed him to make my life a living hell, and I think he readily complied.

One such tryst ended with me suffering a swollen knee from a fall, or more or less a push from the school's staircase. This had to be seen at the General Hospital. I remember the warm gauze they applied along with some sticky substance to my injured knee. All the doctors and the nurses there had remarked on my bravery and were impressed with the many pertinent questions I had been asking concerning their dealings with my knee.

When I reached home that evening my grandmother was livid. The next day she made serious preparations to have me admitted to the nearby Bay Primary School. I was accepted for the September term of 1962. Here began a liaison with the people of the Bay Land, Dunlow Lane and Rebitts Land area.

My first class at Bay Primary was Infants B-1, taught by one Mr. Labourne Sampsom. For the duration of my school days I have had the good fortune to come into contact with teachers who presented themselves as proper role models for their students. Mr. Sampsom was one such individual.

He was a precursor to Mr. Harry Sealy at Combermere School. Never one to fear the administering of corporal punishment, he walked the length and breadth of the school with a strap at the ready for any boy who dared to step out of line. On the other hand, Mr. Sampsom, as in the case of Harry Sealy, was a sportsman. He played table tennis, but was too modest to admit that he was one of the better players of the game on the island. It so happened that one day someone showed us the *Daily News*, and there was Mr. Sampsom on the sports page executing a back hand flick, his familiar features in serious concentration. After this we had a new fondness for him that would last years after our school days had ended.

Infants B-1 at Bay Primary has produced many outstanding citizens in the country. There is Walter Maloney a.k.a. 'Lopey', or 'Bug You'. He is now a leading civil servant and is the President of the NUPW. Then there is Mark Cummings, who is now the Chief Town Planner at Town and Country Planning. Billie Griffith has gone on to become one of the leading hoteliers on the island of Bermuda. David Harper, a footballer of some great ability now resides somewhere in the British Virgin Islands. He represented Notre Dame and turned out as a mid-fielder for the Barbados National Team. Other players of note from Infants B-1 were Andy Wall and Carl Edgar who were also national football players.

Somewhere in between these luminaries are people such as myself who showed so much promise right from the start, but were allowed to deliver so little.

From Infants B-1 we went into Class One. Our teacher was Mr. King. He was another strong disciplinarian who never spared the rod if he thought it would spoil the child. Mr. King loved a drink of rum as much as anyone. It was rumored that the flask he carried in his small suitcase always contained some liquor, and he would from time to time during his teaching take a swig.

Then it was on to Class Two. Mr. Alleyne (my namesake, but we were not related) was an even sterner taskmaster than the previous two, and he was stronger to boot. Mr. Alleyne can be accredited with having afforded me the facility to learning my tables. He carried a short bamboo rod, and would have us repeat our tables right after lunch. As we recited the tables he would patrol between the desks. Whenever he thought he heard a miscalculation he would inadvertently stop the recitations and inquire of the suspected villain to repeat a whole table by himself. If one made a mistake, one would be immediately informed, as a sharp pain cascading down the center of one's back would be indication enough that your calculations needed to be recalibrated.

"Five eights are what?" Alleyne would ask, bamboo raised above his head ready to pounce on any utterance of the wrong answer.

"Forty Sir," the anxious boy would answer and thus save himself from another cut arse.

These sessions have left me with the ability to add, multiply, subtract, and divide with an alarming accuracy. Some may say it was a cruel way to impart learning, but it was effective nonetheless, and it has made me sharp as a razor and quick on the uptake. These are two necessities in today's world that I find lacking among the children of today.

Class Three was taught by a woman—Miss Walcott. Here at last we thought, would be some respite from corporal punishment. No such luck was to be had. Miss Marshall was like a demoness from hell. She made no sport, and indeed we never had any games time as before while we were in her class.

These were crucial times. We were on the verge of taking the Common Entrance Exam, and there was no time to be playing games. Books were the order of the day.

Our class at that time was situated right adjacent to the headmaster's office. Our behavior, our deportment and general hygiene had to be on point. Those were the days when you were inspected each morning by your teachers. Your hair had to be neatly combed, your teeth well brushed, your clothes were to be immaculate and your shoes were required to shine like a bell.

Failure to achieve any of these would result in you having to fall out of the line up and retreat to the nearby standpipe, where some of the older boys would give you a lesson in proper deportment as well as give your hair a combing. After this you would be exercised with simple calisthenics to get your adrenalin flowing for the lessons ahead.

Class Three marked the end of my stint at Bay Primary. This great school (whose predecessor was Bay Street Boy's) had produced none other than the legendary national hero Sir Garfield St. Auburn Sobers. The great man lived in the immediate area (Walcott's Avenue) and any time he was in town we would traverse through the narrow track that led to his house and remain outside his window chatting with this monolith of a sportsman. Humble as ever, he would sit in his side window and engage us in any topic that we carried to him, right up until it was time for us to return to school.

Bay Primary set the motion for my development. It was here that I was introduced to discipline. It was here that I made friendships that would indeed last for a lifetime. Many of my friends are from the Bay Primary and the Bay Land area, which remains to this day one my favorite places on this island. Whenever I return to the area, it's like walking through a time tunnel with the number of faces from the past that I see there.

Bay Primary laid the foundation for my entry into the only other school I ever aspired to attend—that university situated at Waterford.

The Emperor

The year was 1966 and it was the month of April. I was preparing for the Common Entrance Exam. In those years the exam was done in two parts. I had already passed the first part and had embarked on a mission to gained entry into one of the older government schools.

I received extra-curricula lessons given by a Mr. Durant of the Roebuck Primary School. My school at the time was Bay Primary Boy's School.

On evenings I would leave my home at Henry's Lane on Lower Collymore Rock, crossing the road onto the compound of Enmore Health Clinic, and proceed down a flight of steps, which led out onto Martindale's Road. Here I would traverse the length of Martindale's Road in a direction which ran parallel to the Queen Elizabeth Hospital until I came to Taylors Gap, where I would meet up with my friend Arthur Holder and we would continue on past King James Shop which stood on the corner of Belmont, Halls, Martindales and

Constitution Roads. From here we would make our way into Queen's Park and climb over the coral stone wall that separates Queen's Park from Weymouth 'C'.

Next we would wriggle our way somewhere behind the Transport Board Company and into the small jungle at the back of Transport Board. Carefully eluding the two doberman pinchers belonging to the headmaster of Harrison College, we would ease on out through the back gate of the school and onto the precincts of yet another school, this time the Metropolitan High School, and over to the Moravian Church yard on Roebuck Street right next to Lionel C. Hill's Supermarket. The Roebuck Primary School where our studies were conducted was located behind the church.

On one such evening, Arthur and I reached the corner by King James shop, only to find our progress impeded by a host of onlookers who lined both sides of the road. Police outriders were travelling up and down the street, and other traffic cops were diverting all vehicles to the many side roads on Belmont Road.

As far as we could ascertain, someone of great political stature or royal distinction was about to make an appearance. We were quite sure it wasn't the Queen of England, as in those days whenever royalty was in town, we the children were usually given a front row seat, so to speak, and little Union Jacks were distributed to us. When the Monarch passed before us we would smile and wave our flags, the Monarch in return would smile and wave that practiced wave that all monarchs seem to have perfected.

Being completely in the dark as to who the person of importance was, whose passage would warrant such disruption of normal activity, we held our ground and watched as proceedings unfolded. Those were the days when children were supposed to be seen and not heard.

Pretty soon a buzz arose from the large crowd, and the lawmen were working feverishly to maintain some order. It became evident to two small boys, nine years of age that the VIP would be making their way into view in a short while. Suddenly the crowd erupted and exclaimed as if in one voice "He coming, he coming!"

Soon a long white state car came into sight from the direction of Government House, and inside the open back carriage stood a regal-looking black man, short in stature and dressed in a military uniform, that denoted that he was of a superior rank. His tunic adorned with medals of all description. As all monarchs do, he waved to the adoring crowds while keeping a somber but peaceful look about his face. The roar of the crowd made known to us that this man was indeed of kingly character. This was His Imperial Majesty, Emperor Hailie Selasie I, Kings of Kings and Lords of Lords, Conquering Lion of the Tribe of Judah, and he was making his presence felt on the Barbadian landscape. The crowd murmured again with one voice "Selassie man, Selassie man."

Who was this man? Why was a black man in Barbados of 1966 spoken of in such reverent tones by a populace that hitherto reserved this kind of adulation for the Anglo-Saxon Monarchs?

The Emperor was on his way to the Opening of Parliament and to deliver the Throne Speech. The first and only time anyone apart from the Royal Monarch of Britain had done such. At a later date I would have the opportunity to gaze upon photos of the Premier of the day the Rt. Hon Errol Walton Barrow and his government members genuflecting before this Ethiopian Monarch.

It was said that on his departure from Barbados he had made the exhortation "God Bless Barbados." Later in the year, November 30th to be exact, Barbados would become independent. Even later in the following year Arthur and I would pass the second part of our exams and gain admission to the Combermere School.

Combermere School

No one who lived at Combermere Street had attended Combermere School itself. At least not during my life and times there. There were quite a number of lads who lived in the other streets who went to the institution at Waterford.

As previously mentioned, Combermere School was founded solely for the education of the poor man's children. Christopher Codrington had opened Codrington College, which is now a theological institution in St. John. Thomas Harrison, a planter, had sometime later started Harrison College.

Combermere had the distinction of being labeled the 'ghetto school'. It was the normal choice of entry for the poor man's sons.

Long before my time, Combermere had been situated somewhere near the Girl's Industrial School, later known as the Girl's Industrial Union, on that stretch of road that runs behind the Ministry of

Education on Constitution Road (the Old Queen's College building). Later it moved to Weymouth in the building that now houses the Transport Board. Poor construction of its foundation had caused huge cracks to appear on the building, and a decision was made to build a bigger and stronger one at the present site at Waterford.

This was before the National Stadium had been constructed. I began attendance at the school on September 3rd 1967. But my affinity with the lads at Waterford had begun some time before when I used to man the tins on the score board at Weymouth 'C' for them on Saturdays.

At this time I was still attending the Bay Primary Boys' School. My uncle was living at the time in Station Hill, just around the corner from the Glendairy Prison. Whenever I visited him I would sit at his front window and observe the Combermere school bus as it made its way into Bridgetown. My uncle and my grandfather were probably secretly praying that I could summon enough scholastic acumen to gain entry into the prestigious Harrison College, and not become one of these 'Caw'mere vagabonds', as they described them. On the other hand, I would have died if I hadn't been called to Combermere.

On completion of the eleven plus examination (as it was called in those days, even though both parts were taken before the age of ten) one would have had the agony of having to await the results. All eyes in

Henry's Lane were on me, as I was the only one there who had acquired any form of extra tutelage.

Some envious souls had finalised in their minds that this was money wasted on me and that I would continue on my way up to Class Seven at Bay Primary, the price one paid in those days for failing the exam. As the days for the releasing of the results approached, speculation was rife.

Some were given to personally allocating some boys to individual schools, basing their decision solely on how they looked and how they perceived they would look in their respective uniforms. I had been purposely overlooked and no one gave me a ghost of a chance at entering anything else except the Barbados Foundry alongside my grandfather and my uncle who worked there as foremen.

It must be mentioned that these judgments were ill-founded. At Bay Primary I had been quite successful in the three R's. Therefore any such predictions were made more from contempt than from any other rationale that I could readily conceive.

One evening I was engaged in a cricket game on the Federal High School pasture situated at the back of my home, when I heard my grandmother calling me from the confines of her kitchen. Something in the way she sang the two syllables of my name made me abandon my anger at having to leave my game so surreptitiously.

I made my way over the wall that separated my

home from the school pasture.

"Da...vid! Da...vid!" She cooed, and I can still hear her even now, a half century later.

"Coming Ma-Ma!" I replied, my heart thumping like a bass drum.

As I entered the kitchen, I remembered the date. It was June 17th—my birthday. Running through my mind at this time was the thought of having been called to receive some birthday gift before the day ended. Little did I know how right I was to be.

I can remember how as I entered the house everyone present had worn a non-plussed look on their faces, as if to disguise some surprise.

The Merrymen hit song of the day—*Archie Brek Dem Up*—was playing on the radio. My grandmother stood with one of her hands behind her back, and beckoned me with the other one, her eyes brimming with tears. I was in total confusion. Here was this feisty old lady who had weathered many a storm in her time and feared no one alive except God Almighty, standing before me with tears in her eyes.

My first thoughts were that some tragedy had befallen someone close to us, and I haltingly approached, her halfway expecting to hear some sorrowful news.

She gathered me into her arms and presented me with an envelope. The first thing I recognized was the unmistakable Combermere School logo at the top. I screamed knowingly at the top of my lungs, and the entire house burst into congratulations.

"Open it and read it D," my grandmother urged me. I opened the white envelope and removed the letter inside.

"We are pleased to inform you that you have been successful at the Common Entrance Exam, and have gained a place at the Combermere School."

The letter further went on to inform me of the date for my orientation, and for the collection of my booklist. My first form was called Lower One D, far removed from Bay Primary's class titles of Class One, Class Two, Class Three, etc.

This would take some time to get used to.

Caw'mere

My first day at Caw'mere was a tumultuous one, to say the least. I had travelled with my grandmother on the bus to the school and had made the horrible error of taking all my text books with me, only to find out that the first day of the school year was reserved for orientation, receiving your timetable and becoming familiar with your form mates and your form teacher. All this would be over by 11 am, at which point school would go into recess until the next day. So it was with much trepidation that I had to lug my heavy bag of books onto the bus once more and all the way back home without having opportunity to open one of them.

The next day started in full effect with prayers and assembly. The headmaster was Mr. Stanton Gittens a.k.a. Napoleon Bonaparte, a short, gaunt man with a completely receded hairline and a shiny head top that resembled a well-varnished mahogany table. He had at one stage in his life been a radio commentator of sorts until making the unfortunate error of allowing his worst emotions to get the better of his verbal description of a turn of events on the field of play.

Barbados was playing cricket against some other island team in the regional tournament. Barbados was the fielding side and the other side was occupying the crease. Some fast bowler of note had delivered a snorter of a delivery and the batsman, in trying to evade it, had skied an easy catch into the outfield. The fielder in question, brimming with confidence and some complacency, had got himself into position and settled under the descending ball.

Napoleon Bonaparte too had become complacent and automatically believed that the catch, easy as it was, had become a done deal. However, the poor fielder had become distracted by some unforeseen event and ultimately grassed a simple catch. Napoleon Bonaparte had described the play in flowing terms, if not all proper for broadcast in the public domain.

"And the ball goes into the air, the fielder comes around and settles to take the catch."

Bonaparte reported in the knowledge that even his long deceased grandmother could resurrect herself and take a catch as simple as this sitter. But when the unthinkable occurred Bonaparte made the unperceivable error of exclaiming: "Jesus Christ, the fucking idiot drops the blasted ball!" And that was the end of Stanton Gittens, as a commentator, that is.

I can now relate this event from the safety of manhood, for to mention this while being a pupil of Combermere School would be to ask for an automatic whipping. My first whipping came on the second or third week that I had spent there. It happened in some rather unforeseen circumstances.

I had begun to observe that when the bell that signaled the end of the lunch period had sounded many of the boys from the older school would ignore it for a few minutes before making any move to re-enter classes. I had come to believe that this practice was a normal occurrence, and one that sat well with the authorities of the school. The error of my thinking was soon to be revealed to me in an immediacy I could not have foreseen.

One morning in the hall after prayers, the headmaster took note of this practice and decreed that anyone found loitering on the school pasture or the corridors after the sounding of the bell would be on the receiving end of a whipping.

Lo and behold!

That same lunch time, we decided to play a game of 'catcher'. One person would hide a belt, and ask the rest of the players to search for it. The one who stumbled upon it would ultimately become the new catcher, and the others would run like hell to escape the catcher's lash. Any unlucky soul who suffered such fate would automatically catch the 'virus' of the catcher.

I had stupidly volunteered the services of my belt. This was a gift from my mother who at the time was still residing in jolly old England. She had sent me a belt made of genuine leather and made resplendent with 007 logo, and the accompanying image of Sean Connery, the James Bond of the day, adorning the buckle. This was as close as to a novelty piece of accessory as one would get in those days, and one that I dare not return home without.

In a while the bell rang signaling the cessation of the forty-five minutes we had for lunch. Still my belt had not been found. The concealer immediately made his way to take his seat in his form room, leaving me all alone on the pasture in full view of the headmaster, who watched in interest as I searched frantically for my possession. What seemed like a lifetime, but probably was no more than fifteen minutes, had elapsed. All the while Napoleon Bonaparte continued his vigil, as apparently I would become the first offender to flagrantly disobey his command.

The quandary I was in was of confusing and gigantic proportions to say the least. If I were to return home without my belt I was sure to raise the ire of my uncle, explanation or no explanation. It would be my uncle's leather strap and my behind. Talk about being between a rock and a hard place. So I decided to chance my hand by ignoring the headmaster's orders, a decision I soon regretted.

Finally I discovered my belt, replaced it around

my waist, and proceeded to gain my entrance to the form room without detection. Bobbing and weaving like a prize fighter, I traversed across the now empty corridors. By now the entire school had been ensconced in their respective classrooms, and classes had begun in earnest. Yet here I was like the boy who stood on the burning deck when all but he had fled.

"Sonny! Follow me!"

An authoritative sounding voice boomed from behind me. I turned to see the dreaded face of Napoleon Bonaparte showing me the way to his office. The inevitable was about to occur. It made no sense trying to explain or appeal. The die was cast.

And so within less than one month of gaining entry into Combermere I was asked to bend over and place my hands on the handles of a cane-bottom chair, and have my bottom caned, three bolts of electric shock bringing tears to my eyes, more from embarrassment than from the pain itself.

Harry Sealy

Harry Sealy was a gem of a man. He taught mathematics to the junior school. Harry Sealy never sent anyone to the headmaster or placed anyone in the after-school detention. But he was not one to be trifled with. He was a patient man, but one who would readily give you a piece of his mind if you happened to run afoul of his high standards of honesty and forthrightness.

Had I gained acceptance to any other school in the secondary school system, I probably would have gained many advantages. But one disadvantage would remain glaringly before me for all my days. I would never have collided with a teacher who possessed all the attributes necessary to mould young people into outstanding citizens.

Harry Sealy totally eclipses any memory I have of any of the other teachers I had met at my first school, Bay Primary Boys'. It is my firm belief that every young boy under the age of thirteen should at some time in their young lives come into contact with Harry

Sealy, much in the same way as I had. Had this been a natural event in our life and time I firmly believe that this world would no doubt be a much better place.

Mr. Sealy not only taught mathematics, he also taught one about the hard cold facts of this sordid affair generally called life, and all its drawbacks. He offered solutions to life's many problems, and he placed great emphasis on shaping our lives in order to take our rightful places in the scheme of things, and achieve our goals in this existence. He was your friend and your father figure during school hours. When he was around you felt safe. You believed that you could accomplish anything that you set out to achieve. His mere presence gave you the confidence to shine.

Mr. Sealy was a sportsman *par excellence*. It was rumored that he had formed some kind of alliance with the late Sir Frank Worrell as boys, and they both took on the might of local First Division cricket, and conquering them to bring home the Division One Cup for Combermere School. There is a photo that stands on the wall of the school hall, which shows a team that includes J.E.D. Sealy (a former West Indies player), Sir Frank Worrell (a former West Indies captain), Mr. Stanton Gittens, Mr. Harry Sealy, and one other West Indies player, Mr. Peter Lashley. Harry Sealy and Sir Frank are seated in the front row of the photo and right between the both of them is the Division One Cricket Cup of Barbados.

On our games day, Mr. Sealy would multi-task as

umpire, coach, captain of both sides and mentor when we were playing cricket. In the football season he would be the referee for the game, and he would instruct any potential he could envisage amongst us. He was a colossus of a human being.

The last time I saw Harry Sealy was years after I had finished school. It was one of the annual reunions held by the school's alumni. It was the only one that I had attended at the time. We saw him standing in the foyer outside the school's hall, where the celebrations were taking place. One by one we gathered around him and greeted him. He had become by this time virtually blind and his spine had acquired a rotundity that appeared to make him look shorter than we knew him.

Despite his obvious afflictions he was as jovial as ever. His trademark thick, black moustache and the mole on the side of his face, along with his ever present Ray Ban sunglasses, brought back memories of our days at school under the tutelage of this great man. The remarkable thing that stands out from this our final meeting was the ability to decipher every voice and identify us by name, even though he was robbed of his sight.

The final rites he performed among us were the most moving thing I have ever experienced. When he was about to take his leave of the function he signaled us to once more gather around him and instructed us to place our hands upon his. When we had done as he had instructed, he placed his other hand on top of the pile of limbs and quietly said to all of us:

"Fellows, just remember all Combermerians must stick together."

In less than a year after this, Mr. Sealy was fittingly honoured at a dinner function held to commemorate the tri-centennial anniversary of the school. He died shortly afterwards. He was a man who, for as long as I live, I will always hold dear in my heart. This one had taught me not only to be a man, but to be a man of integrity.

I can hear the question resounding on every lip: What does all this have to do with Nelson Street? Well, here goes. Napoleon Bonaparte was a frequent visitor to the area, for what purposes I cannot tell.

Mr. Sealy carried a striking resemblance to Mr. Tonic Prescott, the owner of the New York Club night club, and both exhibited a certain calmness about them that usually belied the storm lurking underneath. If driven to the brink, they would say their piece and then revert to silence.

Lord Combermere had founded the school and donated it to the education of the Negro slaves and their offspring. Therefore Combermere had the distinction of being referred to as the 'ghetto school'. It was for this reason that I had secretly prayed that I gain acceptance to no other school on earth. Indeed many of my friends who had come from the area gained admittance to this prestigious institution at

Waterford.

But the most striking and visible connection to the school was situated between Wellington and Bay Streets—a street that carries the unmistakable name of Combermere Street.

The Senior Years: Up and On.

My first form teacher, just like my last class teacher at Bay Primary, was a female. Her name was Miss Rochester (later to become Mrs. Dorien Pile, the first female principal of the school). She was an affable young lady and made us feel at home immediately. She taught us Geography, and had selected me to be the form monitor.

Of the other teachers I can remember clearly, there was Mr. Brathwaite, a stout-looking gentleman who ran the bookstore, and who also had a son among us. He was short of stature, and gentle by nature. He taught us English Language and History. During History he made us read the text, and as I sat at the head of the class, he called on me more frequently to open the proceedings. This bothered me none, for I had always been an avid reader from the time I could speak. It was History that enlightened me the most— reading about ancient civilizations I had never heard mentioned before. My interest was piqued, and I now had something to research further when I went into the Public Library on weekends.

I was now entering the historic world of the Turks, the Persians, the Anglo-Saxons of the Great China Wall, the Trojan Horse, and Phididipides the marathon runner who ran from Athens as a messenger and dropped dead on his arrival. It was a new and exciting world opening before me and I thoroughly enjoyed it. Now I could converse with the seamen when they returned from their world wide travels. They in turn were astounded at the ease with which I could rattle of the names of any country on the map along with their respective capitals.

I owe all this to Mr. Brathwaite and his history lessons, and coupled with my Geography tuition from Miss Rochester, I was equipped to make my mark on the fact finding landscape of historical research and analysis in this new world I was now discovering.

My music teacher was none other than the illustrious Dr. John Fletcher, that renowned organist who played at St. Michael's Cathedral. He was a stern taskmaster as he thought that we had possessed some musical potential but were too lazy to fully exploit it. This frustrated him no end and he would administer several thumps to any part of our anatomy he seemed fit. This led many boys to stay away from his classes. But he was adamant that we should be musicians. I dare say that much of what he taught us then went out of our nervous heads. However, later on as I re-entered the world of music I started to fully comprehend the meaning of his teachings. Now many of my alma mater would find it inconceivable if they were to hear me report that I am eternally grateful to Mr. John Fletcher and Mr. James A. Millington, who was my violin teacher. Even though they were rough, their teachings have made my understanding of the art of music so much easier.

Religious Knowledge was taught by no less a person than Napoleon Bonaparte—the headmaster Mr. Stanton Gittens. It took us approximately two weeks to decipher that the man who stood on the platform on mornings during prayers, and who occupied the glass encased office at the front of the school, and the one who taught us Religious Knowledge were one and the same person. When this revelation was made to the other lads I had already received my first whipping at the hands of Mr. Bonaparte. After our discovery we resisted the urge to be noisy and boisterous in his class ever again.

My mathematics teacher slips from memory, as this was a subject that no matter how hard I tried I never seemed to fathom. Every problem, every equation gave me so much difficulty that I had considered dropping this subject from this early in my academic career.

Spanish was taught by one Chesterfield Phillips, who had told us he moonlighted in his spare time as a

Citizen's Band operator. What he didn't tell us, but this was later divulged by some of the older boys, was that his nickname was Bombero, the Spanish for fireman. Indeed the first Spanish text book we did was called *El Lobo del Calle*, and there was a character there called: you guessed it—El Bombero. When the time came for one of us to read the text in particular, the task fell on the class clown Phillip Bellamy. Bellamy was a regular comedian and would have us cracking up with his St. Lucy accent and his country mannerisms. When Bellamy reached the part with the word 'bombero' in it he said the word with so much emphasis that the entire class tried unsuccessfully to suppress their laughter. Bombero was not amused, but we certainly were.

Those initial days at Combermere were of mixed emotions. Some days things were dread, especially when drastic measures were necessitated to exact the desired discipline from the lads. At such times Mr. Bonaparte would become like Pharaoh and read us the riot act in no uncertain terms.

The school rules said you were not allowed to remain in your form room during the luncheon interval; you were not allowed to run along the corridors at any time, you were not allowed to abscond from playing games without the assistance of a medical certificate from a licensed doctor fully stating the cause of your non-participation. But the main school rule that held our interest was the one that read: A breach of common sense is a breach of the school rules.

We travelled on through school uninterrupted until we reached fourth form. Along the way I had been given a scare when in Upper One B my grandmother died, leaving a void in my existence. Until that time she had been my buckler and my shield, my comforter and the mainstay of my young life. On the day of her funeral I was left like a boy marooned on an uncharted island all alone. She had forewarned of this eventuality many times beforehand, but in my youthful exuberance I had ignored her words of wisdom, and on that sorrowful day, inconsolable and heartbroken, I had cried like I never cried before.

Needless to say my studies suffered at this point and I had to be reminded in a timely fashion that if I didn't buckle down and do better, I would soon be joining the ranks of the superannuated. I plunged into my school work with a passion that alarmed even my mother who had returned from England to take the place of my grandmother. And then it was from one extreme to another, as everyone was now saying that they felt I was studying too much for someone my age. However, I was undeterred, as my primary focus was to regain the ground I had lost since my advent to the school. My grades began to show improvement and my teachers were impressed for the most part.

It was at this juncture in my life that I came into contact with Mr. Harry Sealy. He helped me through my infelicities and provided a one-man support system for me when everyone else had lost faith in my ability. With his assistance I completely bludgeoned the promotion exams and catapulted myself into second form in a blaze of glory.

Third form was uneventful in the least. The only thing I can remember from those hazy days of thirteen was the untimely death of the Great Jackie Opel in March 1970. This had left me crestfallen, for this man was my musical hero, and to boot, my mother had given the money along with the permission to attend his upcoming concert to be held at the Globe Cinema.

I had gone early that morning onto Bay Street by the open window with my school mate Bert Riviera, and had seen first-hand the mangled remains of his sports car, and his bloodied body parts in the road. It was an unbelievable sight and we were still in doubt that this was the great man, even though we could see that this was his car, all twisted and wrecked before our eyes.

At fourth form another tumultuous occasion offered itself to me. A young lady I had been dating had jilted me for another. I had taken her love for granted and when the end had come I was in denial. But then reality had struck me like a ton of bricks, and I went into a tail spin. I became lackadaisical in my approach to studies. This was my response to a broken heart. This time there was no Mr. Sealy to rely upon and so I had to forfeit my entry into fifth form.

Just as I had done at Upper One B, I rebounded and again blasted my way towards promotion. But the damage was done. My birthday fell before the end of the school year, and so by the beginning of the ensuing year I would have reached the age of eighteen and so my school days were about to come to an end. I made use of the little time I had left and set about to acquire passes in the few subjects I knew I could master properly. And so on July 1975, I exited Combermere School, leaving a trailer load of memories behind, enough to last me until the day I die.

I consider it a privilege and indeed deemed it an honor to be amalgamated with this great institution, which has produced some of the most illustrious sons and now daughters of this coral stone isle.

Part Four

Jewelina

Jewelina woke up early that morning. The sun had just peeped through her window, and the morning birds had begun to sing their early bird melodies.

The street lights were still burning, but it was evident that a new day had dawned. Jewelina turned in her small bed and took a cursory glance at the little crib next to her. As if on cue, little Kirani started to whimper in his sleep, and then out of nowhere he began to cry just like that.

Kirani was seven months old. He was Jewelina's pride and joy. Even though she had endured the nine months of pregnancy all on her own, she brought Kirani into this world one cold Sunday morning on the maternity ward at the General Hospital under the watchful eyes of the doctor and two nurses on duty. It had been an uncomplicated delivery, just as the entire pregnancy had been uneventful. He was her very first child and she had made up her mind, as she laid eyes on him that first time, that she would move heaven and earth in order for this little bundle of joy to have a decent life in this God-forsaken world.

At the very moment Kirani had entered the land of the living, the man who had sired him, and whom he would never come to know as his father, was just turning over to plant a kiss on the forehead of his lover. A short, innocent-looking girl of no more than seventeen years stretched her adolescent body across the length of the bed and sleepily announced: "Ah sleeping." Her accent was one of those that nowadays seemed to pervade every square inch of the island of Barbados. A definite tinge of Dutch influence could be traced in her intonation, and her Mayan Amerindian features lent proof to the fact that she was a Guyanese lass.

Jewelina took the small boy out of the crib and began to soothingly coo sweet nothings into his ears. Kirani was adamant that with the absence of any other form of alarm in the small one-bedroom house, he would make it known to everyone within earshot that morning had arrived.

The harangue that the baby boy made awakened his grandmother, and she immediately alighted from the bed she shared with Jewelina, making her way into the yard to perform her early morning ablutions.

Annabella was a young woman, even though she was seven months into being a grandmother. She had given birth to Jewelina at an early age, as Jewelina had given birth to Kirani; all before their fifteenth birthday. Both had been saddled with the misfortune of having to bring their offspring into the world minus the companionship of the men who had impregnated them. They had both been left with the burden of sustaining their young charges on their own, as the philandering sperm donors had absconded after receiving the news that they were about to become fathers.

The only difference between the two scenarios was that Annabella's St. Lucian mother had kicked her onto the streets for embarrassing her. She had gone out on a limb to bring Annabella over from St. Lucia to Barbados with the expectation that she would make use of the opportunity, and grasp a solid Barbadian education.

But alas, Annabella had been caught up with the wrong crowd. Boys and parties had been her main interest in those days and eventually the inevitable occurred. She became pregnant for the captain of a shrimp trawler.

Her mother was so angry on discovering her predicament that she had violently confronted her, and made sure that everyone knew that she was not pleased with how her daughter had treated her assistance.

"Annabella!!" She screamed, placing emphasis on every syllable of the girl's name. "Annabella!" she repeated, this time louder than the first. "Annabella!

How many times I call your name, heh? After all the sacrifice I make to bring you over here to this country so you could get a proper education, you gone and shame me so?"

Annabella had closed her eyes to reduce the stinging of her tears. Her world, which only a few weeks ago seemed to be one of roses and bloom, suddenly cascaded into despair and frustration. Her obstinate ways paid her in full, and as she stood under the accusatory glance of her mother, right then and there she knew that things were about to change, and not for the better.

"Well let me inform you Miss Thing, there will be only one woman in this house."

Her mother's thick St. Lucian accent reverberated through her head, as she smelt the impending sentence about to be handed down. She had called on her inner strength, and for the first time in her young life she sent a silent prayer up to the One on high, beseeching forgiveness from Him; it was clearly evident that from her unrelenting mother, no such benevolence would be forthcoming.

"When I come from work don't let me find your backside inside this house. You hear me Annabella?"

Annabella hung her head in shame, and listened as the front door slammed with an explosive bang; a firm indication of her mother's boiling rage.

Benjie was a roughneck. A hardened criminal by the age of eighteen, he had seen more battles than

Adolph Hitler, Winston Churchill and Fidel Castro all combined. His was a life of one encounter after another. Some had prophesied that his life's end was fast approaching, and that it would be a bloody affair to boot.

Benjie was the epitome of a ghetto struggler. Born in the Ashby Alley side road of Nelson Street, he had been rejected and evicted so many times in his lifetime that Her Majesty's Prisons had been one of his longest fixed places of abode.

With the advancing years, he had tried his best to earn an honest living. But try as he might, society never let him forget his many years of incarceration at the Green Gates Hotel on Station Hill.

Benjie had haphazardly embarked on a venture of selling snow-cones. And so he had constructed a snow-cone cart on his own, utilizing the carpentry skills he acquired during his many sojourns inside the walls of Glendairy Prisons.

The whole of Nelson Street had patronized his business, and everyone would wait anxiously for his arrival every midday. His cart was spic and span. Benjie, despite the criminal he was supposed to be, practiced high hygienic standards. His business was given another lift when it was discovered that there was none to match his produce when it came to flavor and taste.

Many school children would gather patiently around his cart to purchase one of these delicious thirst quenchers, and he was soon one of the favorite sons of the area. Whereas before he was the symbol of ghetto failure and desperation, Benjie had turned his fortunes around, and indeed his life had taken a turn for the better, to the admiration of the entire community.

Benjie saw Annabella on that evening for the first time. She was sitting beside the stand pipe on King William Street, and her tear-stained face told him that she was a damsel in distress. He could see by her protruding mid-section that she was some months pregnant. Beside her sat a small bundle, which he had surmised contained all her earthly possessions.

"Young girl, you live 'bout here?" Benjie inquired softly.

Annabella raised her head to survey this short man, quite muscular in body, and with a face that denoted he was a man of full maturity. At first she had thought of rebuking him for interrupting her meditations with his interrogation. But something told her to tread cautiously with this one. After all, it was one such of these species that had landed her in this predicament and fled. She watched him for a few seconds, and then the voice of reason had met with her inner conscience and she relented from her initial position of apathy against this man.

"As a matter of fact. I don't even know where I will be living after this day," she answered, and then became annoyed with herself for so easily letting her vulnerability become exposed.

Benjie came closer to her and smiled warmly. Something about the way he smiled made her feel at ease despite the wretchedness of her situation. As he drew nearer she could smell the Old Spice cologne he was wearing, and stole a quick glance at his neat attire. He had the look of a poor man, but one who paid much attention to his general hygiene and deportment.

Gradually she let her guard down. Benjie, sensing this, sought to make her feel at ease in his company.

"Can't live by the baby father?" Benjie asked again.

This raised Annabella's ire and this time she spoke in an accusing tone of voice.

"Wunna men does care 'bout women after wunna get wha' wunna want and de poor woman get pregnant and homeless eh?" This tirade had burst the dam and she began to sob inconsolably.

Benjie realized that he had to do something quickly, or else she would give rise to sending him away. Without a second thought he sat beside her and placed his arm around her shoulder, soothingly rocking her to and fro. When he spoke again, his voice took on the sing-song pattern of a Catholic priest conducting early morning mass.

"Don't worry; stop your crying and come with me. I'll lend you a room for the night."

Suddenly she exploded in rage again.

"You see my condition? What good one night's rest could do me? When I wake up in the morning this baby will still be inside 'o me, and then what?"

"We will cross that bridge when we come to it."

Benjie offered his hand in assistance. At the same time he took the bundle and with one swift movement, slung it over his shoulder. She felt she had no choice. At least none that she could envision right away. Slowly she took Benjie's hand and rose to her feet. She sent another silent prayer above. This time she asked God not to let this man use and abuse her as that scoundrel of a shrimp boat captain had done.

Annabella looked into her grandson's eyes as he lay crying in the crib, where Jewelina had replaced him, having found no way to make his wailings cease. Just like magic, as soon as Annabella had reached with outstretched hands, little Kirani had stopped his crying.

"Come to grandma," she cooed and Kirani stared at her in amazement at first and then reversed his wailings into chuckles of merriment, arms and legs kicking with glee.

"Yes, Y...es come to grandma. Y...es come... to... Grandma."

Jewelina felt a tinge of jealousy creeping up her spine at first, but this soon turned into affectionate adoration, as she observed the perfect union of two separate generations. Her eyes moistened when she remembered how her mother had narrated to her of the trials and tribulations she had to endure in her younger days as a pregnant mother.

Annabella had decreed inwardly that the treatment her unforgiving mother had meted out to her would not be reciprocated to her own daughter and certainly not to her precious grandson.

Jewelina had got down on her knees that morning and asked God to help her impress the people at her interview that morning. She had made an application to a government office for a job as a clerical officer. She had seen the job advertised in the local newspaper. When she checked, her six 'O' levels had been more than enough to entitle her to the opening. She had attained passes in Bookkeeping, Shorthand and Typing, Principles of Accounts, along with English Language, History and Mathematics. But she knew there remained one unrelenting factor that stood between her and the acquisition of such prestigious employment.

She took a shower in the bath in her yard and then proceeded to pamper her lovely self to the best of her ability. Carefully she applied her makeup, making sure to avoid applying it too generously. Then she framed the outlines of her lips with her lipstick, taking pains to avoid smudging by pursing her lips a couple of times. She then surveyed her handiwork in the small mirror that stood before her, convinced that she had done all she could to fake an appearance as a young girl of means as opposed to her more genuine standing of a young girl who came from one of the most underdeveloped parts of the island, and a 'Red

Light District'.

She placed her documents in her hand bag and took a final glance at her pride and joy as he lay sleeping.

"Jewelina? You still here? You gine be late for the interview."

"I heading off now mummy." Jewelina answered on her way out of the door.

"Good luck... put God in front in everything you trying to achieve and yuh can't go wrong."

"Thank you mother."

Jewelina and her mother had forged an inseparable bond between the two of them after Benjie had succumbed to the temptation of crack cocaine and turned away from his self-imposed obligations.

For some time Benjie had shown Annabella that he would be there for her through thick and thin. During the construction of the Bridgetown Sewage Project he had used his snow-cone cart as a refresher to the thirsty workers. He became so friendly with each of them, that they actually threatened the Canadian Bosses with industrial action if they didn't find employment for him on a full-time basis.

The Canadian bosses had fallen in love with Benjie's sno-cones, not to mention his witty jocularity and easy-going manner. So no arm-twisting of any sort was needed in getting Benjie employed at first as a helper. One day he rebuilt a damaged side walk all by himself, and when the hierarchy realized that he had some skill in building, he was promoted to the post of mason. Benjie continued to rise in familiarity and rank among the top brasses of the Canadian firm.

Things were looking bright for Annabella and her infant daughter. She had become the perfect keep-miss for Benjie. She washed his clothes, she cooked his meals, and she cleaned his house and tidied his yard as well as keeping him busy at night with their intimate romantic trysts.

Just when things looked like they were about to burst out onto the open sky, the unfortunate advent of the crack cocaine trade had put paid to Benjie's social advancement. He had become hooked on the 'White Lady' and had deserted his Lucian lover and his adopted daughter.

Right up to the end he had remained a man. Feeling of little or no worth, he had after many unsuccessful attempts at rehabilitation, simply walked away from home, leaving Annabella and Jewelina to fend for themselves in his little abode on Ashby Alley, and took up residence in Crack Land.

Annabella, forever cognizant of Benjie's benevolence in his better days, tried her best to recover his pride and reinstall his industrious ways. But as Benjie sunk deeper into the clutches of the 'White Lady' it became hopeless to even conceive such as a possibility.

Eventually, one day Benjie went missing, and for about two months no one knew of his whereabouts. Not the police, not the pushers, not even the paros*

* paro
   Bajan slang for a drug addict who lives on the street.

who frequented the dope holes with him. No one could give an inkling concerning his disappearance.

Finally one day Annabella was summoned to the mortuary of the Queen Elizabeth Hospital, and there to her horror and astonishment, Benjie lay stone cold on a slab. Dead as a door nail. Annabella had bawled from the pit of her stomach when she saw him, and had thrown herself on his reposed form. The orderlies present had to drag her away and gently removed her fingers from the tight grip she inflicted on the dead man. As she was leaving Annabella screamed his name at the top of her lungs as if so doing would bring him back to the land of the living.

Benjie had been a good replacement for her defaulted parents; he had also doubled as her de facto lover. He raised Jewelina as if she were his own. Benjie sired four daughters of his, all of whom were way past the age of consent. Benjie had plenty of child-rearing experience, and made sure that Jewelina wanted for nothing. Annabella beamed with pleasure the first time she heard Jewelina call Benjie those first two syllables young infants called any male figure their infant eyes could perceive as their one and only male parent/guardian. "Da Da."

Jewelina adored Benjie and Benjie worshipped the ground that she walked on. She would be ecstatic each evening when he entered the house after a hard day's work. Benjie had taken care of her early education and the entire community admired the way he doted over her like a totally devoted father. The only one she had ever known.

Now Annabella would have to explain to her seven year old daughter that the only man she knew as a father would no longer come through that door and pick her up spin her around and around until they both were giddy, and fall safely onto the bed in a loving heap, laughing breathlessly like a pair of troopers.

Any minute Jewelina would be home from her studies at the St. Patrick's Roman Catholic School. She would inquire as she had done for the last two months.

"Ma-Ma, you don't hear from Da-Da yet?" and she would have to deliver the sad news, or somebody out on the road would be only too willing to do the honors for her.

The Politics of Exclusion

"Good morning madam. My name is Jewelina Joseph. I am here for an interview with Mr. Skeete. "

Jewelina was speaking to a young girl, possibly about twenty years old. Her name was Andrea Goddard, as was indicated by the identification card she wore around her neck from a blue ribbon.

"Good morning Jewelina. Welcome to the office of the Ministry of Urban Development." The receptionist said. Her hairstyle was Afro Kinky, but it was neatly arranged on her head and framed her fine features perfectly. Her lips were colored just as Jewelina's own were, in that unmistaken red tone that made even the plainest of women look fabulously sophisticated. Her baby blue outfit rested decently upon her contoured body and was adorned with a corsage of flowers. The presence of her perfume pervaded the room, but not in that vulgar way that the prostitutes on Nelson Street wore theirs. She had an alluring smile that made Jewelina feel at ease.

"Mr. Skeete will see you in a moment. Would you please take a seat and I will inform you when he is ready?"

"Thank you very much," Jewelina replied and made herself comfortable on the fawn-colored sofa situated along the wall. The attitude of the receptionist had made her feel she had already been selected for the job.

After a while the phone on the receptionist's desk rang, alarming Jewelina out of her daydreams.

"Miss Goddard. Has anyone of the interviewees arrived as yet?" The strong voice of a gentleman who spoke perfect English inquired.

"Yes Mr. Skeete. There is a Miss Jewelina Joseph here right now," the receptionist answered.

"Okay, send her right in."

The receptionist stood up and motioned for Jewelina to follow her. She approached a door with the simple sign of 'HR Manager' on it, knocked and waited. In a split second the same gentleman's voice sounded again. "Come."

The receptionist turned the silver door handle that opened the mahogany door. "You can go right in Miss Joseph. "

The office itself was immaculate and air conditioned. Jewelina noticed at once that the temperature here was slightly higher than the one where she had worked at Frere Bentley's Supermarket.

As she approached the desk, Mr. Skeete stood up and extended a well manicured hand towards her.

"Good morning Miss Joseph and welcome," she took his hand in that feminine way that suggested that she was not trying to be too overpowering or too friendly; she gave it gentle shake and then allowed her own hand to return to her side.

Mr. Skeete appraised her composure and took silent note of her general deportment. A smile crept across his face, which put her at ease no end.

"Kindly have a seat young lady."

She settled into a cozy office chair and placed her hands upon her knees the way her mother had taught her to do, especially when in the presence of males. Mr. Skeete waited until she was seated and followed suit. He then took some papers from his desk and quietly perused them. Jewelina began to feel nervous, and a part of her longed for this interview to be over, and to end in her favor. So as not to be detected, she crossed her fingers in one swift motion. Then she sent a silent prayer up to heaven.

"Well! Miss Joseph, I see here you have been educated at the Catholic School. Is that a primary or secondary school?"

"Sir, it is a Comprehensive School," she answered. "We make the transition from primary to secondary right there."

"I see. Your resume looks quite impressive for someone your age."

"Thank you, Sir," she offered. Then she allowed herself to relax a little more and to breathe easier. After a slight pause Mr. Skeete spoke again.

"Now you seem to have the necessary qualifications for this job. So let's see about your general history." Jewelina died a thousand small deaths deep down inside. She thought she knew where all this was leading.

"Ashby Alley. Exactly where is this located in St. Michael?"

She had purposely attached St. Michael at the bottom of her address field, knowing full well that it should have been Bridgetown. She knew that any alley in Bridgetown City would immediately be for all intents and purposes deemed a drug-infested slum by anyone who lived a cozy, middle-class, conservative lifestyle; anyone such as the individual sitting so smugly across from her.

"Just around the corner from Bay Street, Sir," she said, trying to distinguish the vicinity by mentioning one the newly designated World Heritage areas, and stalling the inevitable.

"Hmm. I am quite familiar with the Bay Street area and its historic environs; but this... Ashby Alley can't seem to pinpoint it."

"Well, you have to pass Jemmotts Lane and then turn onto River Road and a few hundred meters to the left, that is where I live."

She evaded, and was becoming slightly annoyed

that she had to lie for fear of not acquiring this all-important job. She felt literally trapped in faking the geographical position of her domicile.

"Is this anywhere near Wellington Street?" He asked the question while raising a quizzical eyebrow at the same time and awaited her answer. Jewelina felt it was time to reveal what she was trying to conceal.

"Yes Sir, not far from there." This was all she could safely offer without giving up her hidden agenda.

"Anywhere near Nelson Street?"

Jewelina felt as if she would scream. She felt like a rat trapped in a corner. She could feel the temples of her head palpitating, and a slight trickle of sweat began to roll down the side of her face. All the composure she had valiantly tried to maintain was now completely gone,

"Not far, Sir." She knew this was no good, but it was all she had left. "It's not exactly on Nelson Street." She attempted this as some kind of damage control.

"When you say not far, please explain my dear."

This term of endearment had set Jewelina on the edge of her seat. She might be from a jungle neighborhood, but she could identify cynical sarcasm whenever she heard it. Jewelina took a slightly more aggressive stance, seeing that her back was against the proverbial wall.

"Does it really matter Sir? You yourself have mentioned that I have the necessary qualifications for the job."

She felt as if she needed to strike out at this self-made bigot, who was grandstanding against her attempt at providing a proper, decent life for her little Kirani. She kept her cool and, taking a deep breath, slowly counted to twenty. Somewhere between seventeen and eighteen she heard his voice again.

"Well as a matter of fact it does. You see we have a reputation to protect and an image to project. We certainly can't be seen to be employing every Jack or Jill who walks through our doors seeking employment. Then our clients might be apt to lose confidence in our ability to perform our duties."

He had spoken with a changed tone, one that was now tinged with contempt. He literally spat the words in her direction. Jewelina was starting to hyperventilate. Her hidden rage was bubbling to the surface. She was trying desperately to be nice to this... man. But she was swiftly losing the battle.

"You see, recent events that have come to light in the media have cast a pale shadow over the area; it has become a kind of a drug garrison, and the law enforcers are having a field day over there with the muggings, the shootings, the murders..."

Jewelina never gave him a chance to finish his sentence. The avalanche came crashing down when he had mentioned 'these felonies' committed in her village, especially when she realized that the persons responsible for the crimes were from anywhere else but Nelson Street.

"Hold it right there. Hold it right there. I don't mean to be disrespectful, but in all fairness, I can't sit here and allow you to heap scorn on my neighborhood by telling lies."

She was beside herself with boiling anger. This was the second or third time she had gone to an interview, and fully qualified, had been intercepted by the prejudices of some Human Resource Manager who had an internal bias against Nelson Street and the people who lived there.

"You ever checked to see who are the ones committing the crimes in Nelson Street?"

She asked, becoming really agitated and animated.

"These people does leave where the hell they come from and come into my neighborhood causing all kind of trouble, and when the police hold them they does say that they from Combermere Street, Wellington Street, Vine Street, King William Street. *Tout mi baki la* from all over Barbados. Sometimes it does be people like you so family come in my village and pick people pocket, rob people, even shoot and murder people, and when done all wunna people does open wunna mout' and wash it 'pon de poor people who striving hard to sen' school dey childrun, striving hard to make ends meet and to pay duh bills, and deprive them of earning a living in this country; all because wunna doan like the people. And then every Sunday morning wunna in church saying how wunna praising God, and how God is a Bajan. I getting tired ah dis kinda thing. I can't tek it nuh more."

She got up from the comfortable seat she had been occupying because in her mind she felt she had overstayed her welcome and no longer wanted to be in this apartheid governmental office, one where poor citizens had to genuflect before the powers that be in order to earn an honest, decent living in the same land that had told her that these fields and hills beyond recall were now her very own. A pack of dirty liars they all were, and the less she had to do with the whole set of them the better it would be for her.

She had made her way halfway out the door when a sudden thought struck her, and if Mr. Skeete thought that he had faced the full intent of her wrath earlier, how wrong he was, for when Jewelina turned to face him again it was if she were breathing fire from her nostrils, and this abrupt transformation actually made him do a double take.

He had never seen a human being in all his time on earth transform so swiftly before. It appeared that Jewelina was about to become physically aggressive, and he had heard that these people from Nelson Street had a great propensity for violent exchanges. Not wanting to be on the losing side of any volatility from such a Nelsonian, he attempted to calm the raging sea that now stood before him.

"This is a government office and I would appreciate it if you kept your voice down or take your leave right now."

If Skeete thought that would be enough to smolder the flaming young girl seething in absolute rage in front of his self-righteous eyes, that was his second big mistake for the day. One that would turn out to be even bigger than the first.

"Lower my voice? Leave right now? I don't think so, not before I have my day in court. So shut up and listen to what I have to say."

She had not intended to be quite so aggressive, but the cool demeanor she brought to the interview that morning had been completely eroded by this manicured piece of filth sitting before her, full of accusation and self-righteous indignation. And so she was no longer in control of her deepest emotions.

"Let me tell you something." She said, consciously lowering her voice but still retaining the same venom in her intonation. "While bigots and racists just like you still go around bashing the folks and may I add the decent folks of Nelson Street, you never even knew of the many illustrious and prominent persons whose navel string were buried there, and who have gone on to make meaningful contributions to this same country that does criticize their neighbors at every turn, to suit their whims and fancies."

Her wide command of the Queen's English had resurfaced from the labyrinths of emotional exuberance to demonstrate the versatility of her communication skills.

"Well, allow me to educate and inform you of the

VIP list from Nelson Street, this same street that you accusing of being a trouble spot. Let me begin by letting you know that years ago even you with your expensive suits and high-falutin' pretentious ways couldn't set foot in Nelson Street. Nelson Street was a well to do area in those days, and scum like you would have been very unwelcomed. Then there were people like..." she paused for dramatic effect, and to give him time to get wind of the message she was about to bring.

"There were people such as Mr. Vic Fernandes, one of the leading broadcasters of the Caribbean, then there is Miss Eudine Barriteau, of the University of the West Indies, and Mr. Clarrie Layne, former headmaster of Harrison College. Then there is Mr. Peter Peters and his brother Julian. Peter is a tutor at the Community College and Julian one of the leading guitar players in the Caribbean. They all come from Nelson Street proper."

She paused again. This time it was to catch her breath, as she was beginning to enjoy watching the look of amazement on this bigot's face when she exposed this list of high end achievers that was beginning to sound like a who's who of Barbadian success stories."

She took a deep breath and continued.

"Don't believe that I am finished. Not by a long stretch. There is Mr. Adrian Clarke, who was the last time I heard, the Head of the Mathematics Department at Springer Memorial School, he used to live on Queen's Street. Then we had Mr. Donald Layne nee Mandeville, and his brother Raymond. They used to reside on Wellington Street, and their mother had a shop on Nelson Street. Don is the Manager of a gas station at Wildey, and Raymond is the owner of Sport's and Games Store. To boot, you see that lovely young lady who is now plying her artistic skills in the US of A and who goes by the name of Shontelle Layne? Well that is Raymond's daughter. Let me continue... Adisa Andwele a.k.a. Aja, he came from the nearby River Road. He is now married to the former Ermine McLawrence, who was born on Beckwith Street and was a leading Banker at Nova Scotia. Yuh getting my drift?"

She paused once more. Now she was allowing him to wallow in his shame before she applied the *coup de grace.*

"Mr. DeCoursey Headley who was employed by Cable and Wireless and then went on to serve as a Customs Guard before his retirement. Mr. Henderson Clarke, another Customs Guard, both of these gentlemen resided at Beckwith Street. And on the field of sports there was Mr. Richard Clarke the captain of the National Softball Team on many occasions, he lived at Queen's Street and is the cousin of Adrian Clarke, the teacher I told you about before. And look at the footballers we produced: Mr. Jeffrey Williams the present Barbados Football captain, Mr. Floyd Bailey, one of the most prolific defenders this country has ever seen, even though these two gentlemen are of

Vincentian parentage. They were born in this country and are full-fledged inhabitants of the area. Then there is Mr. Jomo Brathwaite, another national player of distinction. Let me tell you. The first footballer to score a goal at the National Stadium on its opening was Mr. Andrew Bruno. And now we have the pleasure of counting amongst our people Miguel Cummins, that young fast bowler from the Pondside Housing Development, who now plays for Barbados and the West Indies 'B' team and is on the verge of playing for the senior West Indies team.

"I could go on and on, but I just wanted to demonstrate to you how these people you and all the others like you would like to describe as dysfunctional and idle, are making their presence felt amongst the so-called decent Bajans, and even though you all have ostracized them to some extent, or wunna try to, they have still risen to the occasion to make the area proud. There are so many more waiting in the wings to do likewise, despite whatever you or any one might say."

Jewelina stared at the mortified man sitting in front of her in total shock. And then she exhaled and exhorted: "Have a good remainder of the day Sir." And with that she pivoted and showed herself out.

She didn't give two hoots about this job and had made up her mind to look elsewhere to gain employment in an effort to sustain her infant son and her ageing mother. It was most unlikely to expect after such a performance as the one she had exhibited that she could be accepted there. However, she had said her piece and made her feelings known.

Then one evening, a couple weeks later, the postman delivered a government-stamped envelope to her door. And when she opened it, there was a letter of apology from a Mr. Alexander Mortimer Skeete, expressing his deepest and sincere apology if he had insulted her integrity. And at the end of the letter was an attached note of appointment, slated to begin on September the third. She could not believe her eyes and was beside herself with both relief and overpowering joy. Alas, justice had been served. As her mother had reminded her, there was, indeed, a God.

The Oldest Profession

Wither of these twain did the will of his father
They say unto him, the first. Jesus saith unto
them, Verily I say unto you
That the publicans and the harlots go into the
Kingdom of God before you
For john came unto you in the way of
righteousness, and the publicans and the
Harlots believed him: as ye, when ye had seen it
repented not afterward, that ye
Might believe him.

Matthew Chapter 21, verses 31 & 32

To say that every prostitute is not a whore and that every whore is not a prostitute may be seen by some as a misconception. Definitive evidence is necessary to validate the meaning of this ambiguity.

To understand the substance of this one must first differentiate between the two. Both words are employed to describe a woman of easy virtue who is willing to barter sexual favor in return for legal tender, promise of gifts, and opportunities.

However, on closer inspection, it can be conceived that there is a huge difference between the two, in much the same way there is indeed a difference between a carpenter and a joiner. Even though both may use some of the same tools in the execution of their business, the methodology and the desired result are of separate design. The first can utilize many materials of different quality to reach the zenith of his art form. The second must use only the finest and most expensive materials, and the finish must be exquisite and appealing to the trained eye, in order to exact the highest returns.

Even though both names are loosely bandied around to describe these ladies of the night, as they are affectionately called, each one possesses distinct characteristics and identifiable traits.

The whore, as the mere pronunciation of the word suggests, is of a baser, easier and less expensive construct. Her tools for the trade can be sourced from at the bottom of the food chain. Her elevator needs not to travel all the way up to the top floor, and she needs not be the sharpest knife in the kitchen cabinet. In short, mental stability and intelligence quotient are not prerequisites required for this one to be successful in her chosen field. Indeed it may be less of an expense for to her start up her trade than the more sophisticated prostitute, but her returns will be not of the same quantity.

Her attire alone can be shorter, tighter, more revealing and cheaper than that of the high-end 'hooker'. Thus she will inevitably attract a clientele that is weaker both of pocket and of etiquette, and her sojourn amongst these ingrates might be of a more eventful and incident-ridden occurrence, thereby defaulting any secretion of intent, placing her on the forefront of the flesh trade for all and sundry to behold.

The prostitute, on the other hand, will invariably maintain a clientele of more a mature and conservative nature, thus ensuring that her activities are secret and of a confidential kind. She can dictate when, where and with whom she will be involved, as well as command her price. She may even have to endure the dignified and prestigious renaming process, in an attempt to garner an even higher price for her wares. Ultimately, she may be referred to as a 'call girl', or more discreetly as an escort, etc.

This form of rebranding may seem inconsequential to the casual observer, but might mean the difference of a few hundred dollars, and the comfort of dealing with someone of proper parenting and higher morals, as opposed to being under the weight of some sex-starved, half crazy and intoxicated lout whose sole intention is to make some hapless sex worker suffer indignity all for the measly sum of money agreed upon at the point of entry.

The life of a whore is made even more complicated when coupled with the attachment of certain requirements. In the event that the sex worker is operating from premises not her own, she may be required to give up a portion of her earnings to offset the price of maintaining the establishment where she plies her trade. At such establishments, a time limit is usually given, and any excess might be penalized by the owner, resulting in the whore being saddled with an even smaller pay than usual.

The prostitute has no control, nor is indeed interested in having control over the place of business, except to ensure that it is of reputable standard, and the hygiene of the place is of impeccable maintenance. The whore has no control over such eventualities, and may have to conduct business in the open air, risking life and limb in so doing.

Had Jewelina not gained some sort of employment, she would have been faced with the sordid ultimatum of having to resort to the oldest profession known to man, in a desperate attempt to provide for her baby son and her mother. Living in a red light district would have made this embarrassing in the first place and demeaning in the final result.

Prostitution, the term I shall use from time to time in order to encapsulate the entire sex worker force, can be termed as love turned to hate. It is a starting point for the sex worker to launch her hatred for all men, and for the subsequent revaluation of all of the male species. Ultimately, the whore will assume that all men are of the same lecherous and perverted nature as the ones who mount her body for their daily dalliances with her.

Jewelina was spared this indignity. Many other girls were not as lucky. Having gained no form of employment to support their households, they usually became victims of the sex trade, given the environment and its proximity to the young lady's domicile. With the influx of Guyanese and Jamaican workers who take up residence in the area in an attempt to cut the cost of travelling to and from their places of work, almost every resident of the area can be said to have a neighbor of these nationalities and occupation. Lest you forget, the area is one of the most densely populated in Bridgetown.

Some of these ladies either take the low road of prostitution or the high one of aligning themselves with one of the several drug pushers in the area, and prepare to bear them children, thereby supposedly safeguarding their financial future for a while; this is until the scoundrel lays eyes on a newer and more improved version. Then it is a matter of cat fights between the warring females, fighting for possession of turf and worth.

The jilted most likely will resort to the low road eventually in an effort to maintain her lost lifestyle. All around the area can be seen examples of such females who have had their lives blighted by the culture of drugs and prostitution. Some have placed themselves at the mercy of these felons to accommodate them at their whim and fancy, merely objects of lustful pleasure for these louts of men who masquerade behind their vehicles and jewelry to ensnare and beguile these unfortunate young girls. They are for the most part hunted by these pedophiles from as early as in their formative primary school years.

I am highlighting all this from my casual observations of one of the many social ills I have seen prevail—many a promising young girl, who because of poor choice of spouse has had their potential dashed upon the rocks of drugs and crime, and subsequently marooned into a world of sex and perversion, eventually falling to the dreaded HIV/AIDS and passing on to the great beyond.

Condemnation is not my primary focus here, but rather to assist any young women who may be reading this to take wisdom as their guide when seeking a partner for life, and a father for their child. It is nonsensical of any girl to throw away her future just for the sake of the bling and fling of this dastardly sub-culture. The many beautiful and talented ones I have seen fall victim to this scourge have left me literally with tears in my eyes; for some of them have been my closest friends.

Case Study of a Sex Worker

I had met up with an old school friend outside the Fairchild bus stand one evening while crossing over the Chamberlain Bridge.

We hadn't seen each other since school days, which was some thirty years ago. Our conversation meandered around reminiscing of the good old days of Latin and French and sitting on the old hard bench. We shared jokes about teachers of old, and inquired of each other about many of our mates. On sharing notes, we found out that some had moved into the ranks of the movers and shakers of the country, some yet still had migrated abroad to seek their calling, and sadly, many others had fallen victim to the Grim Reaper.

We surmised that life was for the living and the living was to be done now, before it was too late to have regrets at not having spent time in the pursuit of pleasure and enjoyment. At this point my friend invited me to have a drink for old times' sake, and after much prodding, I eventually relented and accepted.

We made our way down Fairchild Street, still engaged in our animated conversation, oblivious to the standers and the passers-by along the way. As we approached the corner by Cheffette Restaurant, we turned onto Nelson Street.

In those days I had desisted from frequenting the night club scene on Nelson Street as a habit. I was somewhat apprehensive at doing so now, but capitulated when my friend, a country boy, had informed me that he was a staple at the Zanzibar Club, that the ladies there were of Latin American extract, and as he had purported, were as fine specimens of female pulchritude as could be found anywhere.

I climbed the wooden stairs and was immediately entranced by the melodic fluctuations and massive brass line punctuations that describe the sensuous construct of salsa. At the top of the stairs we both paused to take in the atmosphere. I surveyed the room and came up with some pleasing discoveries. My friend was correct in his summation that these women were very beautiful in the first instance, and by their dancing I privately surmised of a fun-loving nature as well.

The ladies were dancing as if they were formally trained in the art of dance. I had given to speculate that their performance was of a more cultural flavor, for at certain points during the musical offering they were

Club Zanzibar
on Nelson Street,
which is still in
operation

given to releasing loud shrieks and the accompanying
"Baila! Baila!"

One young lady not so interested in dancing had
sought to snare me into her world and, rubbing my
back carefully, she spoke with a Castilian accent as she
inquired "Papi, sucky sucky? Fucky, Fucky, eh Papi?"
I politely declined her offer and rested my gaze once
more on the seductive fluctuations of the dancing
mujeres on the floor.

The women were lithe of body and their waistlines
seemed to be designed to make mortal men drool

from their mouths and have little regard for their hard-earned currency.

My friend distracted my attention to direct me over to the bar, where we purchased two Banks Beers and perched ourselves on the high stools situated there.

The Mamasong was a Santo Domingan lady in her fifties who seemed to have been a beauty in her glory days. She served the beers and took our money, all the while tapping her feet gleefully to the music, as she enjoyed the dalliances of the ladies on the dance floor.

As my eyes perused the place I observed that there were other nationalities in the building; namely Trinidadian, Jamaican, a host of Guyanese, and a small helping of local muchachas.

My eyes came to light on one very classy individual who was sitting across the room from me. With crossed legs, upright position, beautiful features and a body most women would give their all for, she presented to me a picture of elegance and sophistication not usually associated with establishments of this kind. She seemed engulfed by the dancing and was immersed in the throes of enjoyment by the performance done in her honor.

She used her peripheral vision and caught me paying more than parochial attention to her existence. She flashed me a brazen smile and blew me out of the water. She was a mulatto by pigmentation, about five feet nine, and her stately presence led one to believe she was some journalist or other, working incognito to gather a scoop on the prostitution trade in Barbados.

She was dressed modestly in a short black mini-dress, accessorised by a pair of red suede stiletto pumps. Her hairstyle was simple, as can be expected for one involved in such an occupation. She had employed the braided extensions that were becoming ever so popular at the time.

Her face carried a look of experience, but it was also framed with innocence that I thought probably belied her years. Simply put, she was an exquisite beauty.

Subtly she worked her flirt on me, and off-camera I could see my friend taking this all in with much interest. She swiftly tossed her long henna colored braids behind her with a swift nod of her head, as if secretly signaling to me that I should follow her into the back, where I was noticing many couples were intermittently retiring.

She smiled at me again, this time the smile reached all the way up to her eyes. This was no commercial smile. I became ensnared, not only by her comely beauty but by something that I couldn't quite put my finger upon, something that allured me to her anyway.

She seized her moment, alighted from her repose, and waltzed over to me in step to every beat of the Spanish music on the wire. Her torso came at me like a torpedo: I saw it coming but there was not a thing I could do about it. As she approached I couldn't help inquiring of myself: *What is a girl like her doing in a place such as this?*

She introduced herself to me, not by mentioning her name, but instead she offered her hand politely. I obliged her by taking it in mine and gently placing a kiss upon a diamond encrusted gold ring I found there. She smiled in amazement. I smelled her Nivea body lotion and a whiff of her Paco Rabanne Cologne.

"Oh! A gentleman!" She exclaimed as she rolled her sparkling eyes to the ceiling and then drops them to meet mine.

"I try to be, whenever and wherever possible." I answered meekly. This woman was reaching into a weaker side of me that before then I hardly knew existed, furthermore that I was in possession of.

Like the perfect hostess, she inquired if I was enjoying the atmosphere, and if I would like to sample some embellishment, as she had observed that I looked a tad bored. Simultaneously she proceeded to massage my bulging trapezium muscles and worked her fingers deftly into my shoulders, releasing tensions I had kept stored for decades.

"There. Feels better now, doesn't it?" I nodded my approval, for indeed she had added about ten years onto my longevity, all in a matter of seconds.

She slowly slid between my legs at the same time, allowing her own legs to mingle with mine. Then she looked into my eyes and I saw her as if for the first time, only this time she was even more beautiful than before. I wondered to myself if I would arrive home safe and alive after all this attention from an angel. Somehow I didn't bother myself with the fact that this could be my final day on this earth and that I was being compensated for all the heartaches and frustrations I had endured; for now I stood before a creation of celestial form and angelic proportions and all this inside the devil's den of lust and fornication.

Paradoxical as it seemed, I was enjoying her company and everyone else in the room had faded into non-existence.

"I like a man who smells good," she leaned over to take in my Perry Ellis and in so doing gave me a glimpse of her ample bosom and its seductive cleavage.

"Thank you very much," I offered.

She buried her head into my chest and slid her tongue between the separations she discovered there. She stopped briefly at my thumping heart and then, using her tongue, she caressed my nipple through the sheerness of the material of the Barclay's Premiere League T-shirt I was wearing.

"Let's go onto the balcony, away from these prying eyes." I got up and sauntered over to the balcony with her, hand in hand.

"Do you live in Barbados?" She asked, shocking me somewhat with the question.

"I most certainly do, my dear. But why do you ask?"

"You look kind of cosmopolitan by the way you dress."

This was probably due to the fact that indeed most of my clothes were gifts from my friends and relatives in the USA and Great Britain, as I had long lost any affection for the haute couture found on Broad and Swan Streets.

"Thank you very much, but I am Bajan to the bone, even though I was born in London England."

"See? I know what I see when I see it."

"Well, I must admit then that you are most certainly a mistress of the obvious."

We tightened our embrace and laughed heartily. Then as if some unseen being had commanded us to be quiet, we languished in our silence for a few seconds. We stared into each other's eyes for what seemed like an eternity, and I saw the moment her lips started to quiver. Our mouths were by now inches apart and our foreheads were actually touching. I could feel this Bajan bombshell beauty falling for me and I as Jill had done for Jack was coming, tumbling after.

"Tell me. What could make someone such as you be in a place such as this?"

I could have kicked myself for allowing my curiosity to make such an incursion into this damsel's personal affairs. But my mind's heart just had to know.

"I have seven children to support and not one of their fathers contributes a single cent to their upkeep. So I must do what I must do to ensure that they have as good a life as any of their friends."

I was slightly taken back by her admission.

"They didn't ask to come here, I brought them kicking and screaming into this world, and the least that I owe them is that I lay down my life so that they might live."

This unselfish contrition impressed me no end, and I unconsciously drew her to me and gave her a light kiss on her cocoa brown forehead.

"Seven children?" I asked. "You don't look a day over twenty-five."

"Thirty-five to be exact," she answered, distinctly watching me for any sign of flattery. "I started bearing children at the age of seventeen."

I admired this young woman's commitment to the upbringing of her children minus their delinquent dads. Something about this drew me closer to her and I gave her a reassuring hug.

"Wanna go for a walk, so we can talk?"

This girl was full of surprises, but I was more than willing to accompany her, even to the ends of the earth. Little did I know that in a few short years I would be called upon to do exactly that.

We walked through Bridgetown hand in hand as if we were lovers for many a year. It suddenly dawned on me that since our meeting in the Zanzibar, daylight has been refused entry between our two bodies.

We window-shopped in Broad Street and stared in admiration at the reflection of ourselves in the show windows of the stores.

At Lower Broad Street we had entered the new Cheffette Restaurant. She led me through the main restaurant and entered a small door at the back of the room. A sign was lit up on the inside of this other room and it indicated for all to see that this was Barbecue Barn. The system here was one of eat first and pay later. We took our seats, with me like a knight in shining armor behaving chivalrously and tucking her chair beneath her, and only being seated when she herself had done so.

After a while a young girl approached us with a hearty welcome and presented us with our menus. She informed us she would return after we had sufficient time to make our respective orders.

She studied the menu with avid interest, and I couldn't help noticing her lovely features, which in my humble opinion could match and very well surpass any of the Latin Americanos at Zanzibar.

"Don't be worried, I'll pay for this one, if you promise that on the next date, the bill will be all yours." This angel of a woman breathed in my direction.

"Oh! I can get this." I defended stoutly.

"On the contrary, I insist, as long as you don't fall from our arrangement."

"So there will be a second date?"

"That depends on you. If you play your cards right there could be many more."

"I feel so cheap, not paying for this one."

"Well, just remember that when it's time for you to pay for the second one." She shot back gently.

And then I realized that we had spent the better part of an hour together, had shared intimate details of our lives with each other and had come to the point where we almost kissed, but nary had given thought to any kind of formal introduction. I leaned forward and spoke in hushed tones, for my words were for her ears only.

"Oh, by the way my name is David, but my close friends usually call me Scotty."

"I thought you would never tell me your name. I thought for a minute I was dating a wanted man who wanted to remain incognito."

Everything about this woman astounded me. Imagine finding a person of such impeccable manners and with such an eloquent command of the Queen's English, not to mention beauty beyond all reckoning, in such a flea bag establishment as the Zanzibar.

At this point the waitress arrived at our table and stood ready to take our orders. My date ordered steak done medium to rare, and I ordered the mahi-mahi, barbecued and garnished with a pasta salad that the menu had indicated was complimentary.

"Will you be drinking anything?" The waitress inquired quite professionally.

"I'll have a glass of wine. Douglas Hill, if you please."

"And what it will be for you, Sir?" she smilingly asked.

"Make that two Douglas Hills."

And with that the waitress sashayed her way into the kitchen to deliver our orders and allow us to further solidify our acquaintance.

When the waitress was out of sight my date gave me that sultry look I was just becoming accustomed to and huskily voiced: "David my name is Waveney, but my close friends all call me Whitney. Please don't ask me why cause I just don't know."

"I guess to be on the safe side then I better do the same and call you Whitney as well." I joked.

"Have you been here before?"

"No. Actually, I didn't even know the place existed before now."

"More of a greasy spoon then, are you?" She was referring to the Main's restaurant and its normal helping of fried chicken, roti and burger servings.

"Okay! You got me. That's one of my vices. I love eating." She raised a quizzical eyebrow and flirted.

"Do you mean that in the literal sense or...?" Before I could answer she continued with: "Forget that I asked that, that's quite out of order to ask."

Finally the food arrived, and I couldn't help noticing that the presentation was of a five star nature. As we were about to eat a wine steward appeared pushing a trolley laden with glasses and a bottle of Douglas Hill wine. He poured our wine meticulously, taking care not to disturb us we ate. His duties over, he wheeled the small trolley away and disappeared behind the curtain that separated the kitchen from the main dining area.

I watched Whitney as she ate. How she controlled the knife and fork with minute precision, cutting her steak into small pieces and gracefully depositing them into her luscious mouth. She caught me staring and quietly queried.

"What's wrong? Why are you staring at me like that?"

I could have sworn that I detected a tinge of American accent; but my mind at this stage was way off making of any precise judgments, so enamoured I had become from being in the presence of this Bajan Mona Lisa.

"You are so beautiful that I find it hard to take my eyes off of you, that's all."

"Eat your food. Maybe then your sanity will return."

"I guess you can say I'm falling crazily in love with your charming display of social etiquette."

"Don't be fooled by my chosen profession. My parents brought me up in the most decent way possible under the circumstances."

"I don't doubt that for a second, my dear, I can see your finer qualities shining through."

"Thank you very much. Now drop the compliments and taste the food. It might soon get cold and go to waste." She joked, and then added: "Don't forget that this time the bill is on me."

The Courtship

The next four dates were affairs of the heart. We watched *Titanic* at the Globe Cinema. We went on a picnic along the entire east coast line. We spent a weekend holed up at the Great Escape and finally we had a family get together at Browne's Beach one bank holiday. Here I got to meet her children for the first time, and the first thing that impressed me about them was their resemblance to their mother, almost to a 'T'.

As the days progressed we became an item on the streets. Whitney had hardly released my hand or removed herself from by my side all this time. We were loving each other, as opposed to falling in love with each other. We loved each other with our hands, our eyes, our hearts, our lips and our mouths and everything else we could find to express our devotion and commitment to each other. Suddenly I realized that 'love' was a feeling that no words could describe.

It could only be felt by two people who thought the world of each other.

We would sleep together sometimes at night, and Whitney would on occasion awake in the middle of the night and announce "David. I love you." And I would in turn reply the same way every time; even though deep in the throes of sleep. "I love you too, baby. "

And when the morning came we would awaken once more, this time to celebrate our love in more tangible form with the accompanying moans, and kisses and screams as we climaxed together, only to lie spent for the next hour.

It was a honeymoon of sorts, but not all about sex. We made plans for the future; how she would leave the flesh trade and set up a cottage industry at home; and I would work in my profession as a construction painter to help maintain her kids.

She had instructed me that if I was to be her man, I would have to assume and share the responsibility of raising her children. And as if to solidify this position, one evening she assembled them before me and exhorted me to deliver a motivational orientation to them.

They listened with silent interest to my counsel, and for the most part they fully accepted my facsimile approach as replacement father, seeing that their biological fathers had usurped their God-given roles in a vain attempt to spite their mother.

Now she was with me, and I felt love like I never felt it before. Even in my sleep.

Even her children were acutely aware of this, and her eldest daughter Tameeka would oftentimes coyly remark, "Mother, you are in love!" Jason, her eldest son showed his pleasure in my presence. He would speak to me in low tones, and had the uncanny habit of averting his eyes when doing so. At first I put this down to his concealment of some grave issue from me, and I had believed that this was negative for the most part.

However, Waveney assured me that he was very respectful and loving towards her and that despite his size (he towered over me and was broader at the shoulders) he was a humble seventeen year old, and never gave a day's trouble in his life.

After a while I realized his mother was correct in her assessment of him. He was handy around the house and was more than willing to run any errands. He had that look in his eyes that said if any man dared to mess with his mother, he would transform Arnold Schwarzenegger style and terminate the bastard without a second thought.

She made good on her promise of abandoning the flesh trade, and pretty soon we had established a cottage industry of sorts from the confines of a rented one-bedroom chattel house. The children played their part in helping her bake the delicious sweet bread on weekends and we sold snacks and soft drinks on the side.

Later we added a new invention from Wendy and Tameeka: the 'suck-a-bubby'. This was a milk-based drink which was parceled into sterilized plastic bags. They were an instant hit, and along with the sweet bread, we came close to making a small fortune. It was enough to send the children to school and put tea, lunch and dinner on the table.

One evening I happened upon the house a little earlier than usual, and was just in time to hear Whitney asking of her charges their honest opinion of me. Thankful for the good fortune, I quietly stood outside and listened attentively to their replies. I was prepared to take my leave there and then had I heard any negativity against me; to wit that I was unsuitable for their mother.

One by one they had offered their approval of me. Unable to see their faces as they spoke, I couldn't help noticing the excitement in their voices. As I walked through the door they turned their heads in my direction, and the surprise registered on their faces allayed any fears of all this being a prepared performance on their part to cajole me into a false sense of comfort.

Our relationship blossomed and developed to the point where her friends were becoming envious of her new found happiness. Some of them were having trouble finding suitable and compatible partners. To make matters worse, some of them had encountered some unscrupulous men who showed more interest in their teenaged daughters than in them. All these 'low-lifes' wanted was to get a foot inside the door, and eventually force their way in, stealthily creating havoc, mayhem and pandemonium in the lives of these hapless souls.

Many of her friends I found to be carrying so much emotional garbage as baggage that the odor of their luggage was overpowering. Abuse had been a staple in their lives ever since their puberty days, and such had been accepted as a normal way of life for most of them. For most of their lives they had come to expect nothing but abuse from their partners, and would actually demand it from any man they became involved with.

Whitney was a virgin to all of this and because of her drop-dead gorgeous looks, along with her kind-hearted nature, she was prime target for her lazy friends to exploit. Now that I had appeared on her social calendar, they knew that it could not be business as usual. And so right from the start they attempted to tear us apart.

It seemed that our meeting had been set in stone ever since the beginning of time. We had been inching our separate ways towards this union without our ever even being aware. Our journeys culminated with that chance of a lifetime meeting inside the Zanzibar. A meeting I had earlier viewed as happenstance, but as I became familiar with her life's story, I realized that we were destined to meet at some point and time in our lives. Many of her male friends and lovers just happened to be some of my closest friends as well. Even my friend from school days who had led me to the Zanzibar that evening had confided that he himself was at one point madly in love with her during her days at Springer Memorial School.

She had indicated to me that most of her earlier boyfriends had attended Combermere School and that in fact one had impregnated her with her very first baby. She just seemed to have this affinity, or bond if you might call it that, with the boys from Waterford. They in turn had fallen just like I had done, for her vivacious curves and her easy-going nature, not to mention her sensuous charm.

Her female friends were mainly of two kinds. Most of them were under-achieving lay-abouts and hangers-on, who thought nothing of using her as a means to an end. They would exploit her generous nature and her propensity for sharing with others. Her decent and loveable disposition meant that any association with her would result in the opening of doors that originally would have been permanently closed to them. Some of them, I observed, hung around her in the hope of one day having sex with her, and loathed the presence of any male in her life.

When they realized that a humble Rastafarian who had little or no claim to fame in the ghettoised version of climbing the ladder of success was the center of her attention, they proceeded to launch a smear campaign against me and our relationship. However, try as they might, we were inseparable. This only served to draw us closer together, but ultimately it wore down the resistance of our love and we began to harbor suspicions of each other.

Next they set out to prove that I was only interested in her for any financial reward available. We weathered every storm they sent our way. We quarreled, we argued, but we never fought. It was a torrid time for us.

Eventually they found the perfect spoil, and facilitated the entry of a third party, one who came bearing gifts; gifts I could ill afford (God knows I would have given this woman the entire world, if I had it). This interloper tried to force me out of her children's life by providing any and everything he could. He tried to make me feel inadequate and useless in my own home.

The only problem was that all of this could not stop our undying love for each other. Money or no money, we held each other tight at nights and slept as if every night would be our last together.

One night the interloper attacked her at the Zanzibar, striking her with a beer crate along her head. I was not present at the time, and he thinking she was all alone, proceeded to take complete advantage, and to unleash his fury on her in my absence. He got the shock of his life, for one of the first things I had taught her was the art of self-defence just in case she were to be attacked by some abusive bully. She broke a bottle and stabbed him in the neck, bringing a premature halt to his onslaught. He was rushed off to hospital and everyone thought he was a goner, as many had surmised that the laceration was located very near his jugular vein.

She was a true Gemini—cool exterior, but if ruffled could become a raging fury in a split second's timing.

It is sufficient to say that this man's interference was the main cause for our separation. We separated as friends and remained that way until the end. After our break up we still met occasionally to get a bite to eat, or to watch a movie together. Mr. Interloper would follow us all around and by this time I had been relegated to being the outside man.

Soon she was in the habit of constantly falling ill, and after numerous trips in and out of hospital, one day she announced to me that she was tired of living. She beseeched me that in the event of her death, to take care of her children while there was breath in my body. This way of thinking had made me scared, as I firmly felt she was serious. I had pledged my unswerving devotion not only to the welfare of her children, but also to the preservation of her own life.

Pretty soon visits to her hospital ward started to take the form of a circus side show. By this time speculation was rife as to her condition, and rumors were flying left, right and center. I had also been scarred by these rumors, and I was deemed as one who was terminally ill. Even though everyone could see that I was in the pink of health, it mattered none.

On my last visit, I had informed her that I wouldn't be returning. She indicated that she knew me well enough to expect such. It was impossible for me to stand idly by and watch all and sundry arrive at her bedside and keep vigil in the hope of being there when her final moments came. They stood in silence as if willing her to die right before their eyes and before the allocated visiting hours finished. No one seemed interested in relaying not even the slightest ray of hope to my lover, and I seemed to be fighting a losing battle in trying to keep her focused on staying alive.

In retrospect, I can now uncover the hidden agendas of these harbingers. They had been envious of Whitney all along, and had been secretly praying for her early demise, pretending all the while that they had her best interest at heart. This is the symbolic trademark of some of these sex workers—they won't mind paying lip service to the idea of solidarity, but when it actually came to putting words into practice, they would prefer to lose the game by default instead.

Then one day I had heard that she was gone. Things being as they were, it was inevitable, and I had been left with a feeling of guilt over having abandoning her in the end. I cried my eyes and my heart out, and to this day, some fifteen years later, I still wake up at nights hearing her calling out to me. I still see her face in my dreams and in my every waking moment.

My heart was broken into a million pieces, and on the day she was buried, I remained at home sitting on my bed, surrounded by all of her pictures. I viewed this as the only fitting way I could pay my respects to her, and not in some Anglo-Saxon church with a host of hypocrites gaping and gawking over her while castigating her character right into her grave.

To this day I believe that my heart still has a few pieces missing, as I don't believe it will ever beat the same as before. Besides my grandmother and my own mother, no other woman has had so profound an effect as her and I dare say that I think none can ever take the place of this beautiful and sophisticated woman that no one ever really understood. That is, no one except me.

Part Five

Poke

I come here to bat
I en come here to joke
I en come here to make no runs
Cause I come here to poke

As I reach the crease
The run rate gine drop
I might bat for the whole day
But when play done I gine still be nought
I en bound to trouble the scorers
Dem could all drop to sleep
I here to frustrate de bowlers
And dem fielders in de deep

I come here to poke I want you to understand
I en playing one attacking stroke
I playing hand after hand
And don't think you could chirp me
Wid nuh long hop or full toss

I strictly playing to draw
I don't care bout win or loss
If yuh pitch it up
I playing forward
If yuh drop it short
I playing forward still
You could bring in dem fielders
you got in de deep
Well keep dem down there then
Just now they gine drop asleep

I come here to bat
I en come here to joke
I en come here to make nuh runs
Is poke I come to poke
Maiden after maiden
Is how I intend to bat
Dot ball after dot ball
And who vex , well to hell wid dat

Yuh see I got shots granmerrah
But only when I playing in de road
When I out here pon de pasture
I does be in a poking mode
Who vex leh dem vex
Dis is my hand and I batting as I like
Wunna better doan get me vex
Or I might soon appeal fuh light

When I come to this crease
The run rate will start to drop
And if I bat fuh de whole day
My score will still be nought

I come here to bat
I en come here to joke
I en playing one single shot
Is poke I come to poke.

Cricket, Lovely Cricket

Robert Clarke, Alan Ball, Jeremy and Spanner all used to play cricket right outside St. Ambrose Church. The wall of de old General Hospital ran de whole leg side length of the pitch and de bowlers used to run up from de Death Room side.

Poor Miss Muslim house would bear de brunt of de many offside drives. Any on-drives would mean that yuh out. Once de ball went over the hospital wall it was out you out. A steady supply of tennis balls were needed, 'cause when de ball went over by Miss Muslim and she was in a bad mood it would sometimes come back dissected.

These were the happy days of cricket out by St. Ambrose when we used to play hand after hand to warm up. When more players arrived we would pick two teams to play against each other. These were the good happy days of hopping ball cricket.

Richard was a master of most games and he was a

prodigious cricket player. Richard was quite able to dismantle a bowling attack by himself. He was the epitome of style and exquisite stroke play. He was a very intelligent player of spin bowling, but he favored the quick stuff. However fast or spin, if you made the cardinal error of miss-pitching to Richard you paid the ultimate price, as was found out by Robert Clarke one evening. Richard did a Gary Sobers and took six sixes off of one of his overs.

Georgie Catlyn was a fantastic striker of the ball. He was big in stature and was built like a Sherman tank. He was one of the fiercest strikers of the ball I have ever seen, and many times he demoralized bowlers to the point of surrender.

Grantley 'Moss' Clarke earned the nickname of 'Sir Viv' long before Sir Vivian Richards had become knighted. Moss was similar in features to the great man and walked to the wicket with the same swagger. He was a power hitter who could turn the course of an innings in one over. He had excellent eyesight and two good hands trained by his dedication to the game of road tennis. When on the go Moss was joy to behold. But one silly mistake and the spectators would groan in frustration. This was until the next time that Moss was ready to explode.

Jeremy was what Geoff Boycott would call a lollypop bowler. But he was not to be trifled with or taken for granted. He had the ability to deliver five lollypops in one over, and if the batsman didn't take advantage of these gifts, the next ball he would be presented with an unplayable flipper that would take his wicket.

As I said before, Robert Clarke and Alan Ball were fierce competitors and had many a ding dong battle complete with sledging, name-calling and any other distraction they could find up their sleeves to gain that edge over their opponents. It was street entertainment in its purest indigenous form.

Street cricket gave one the opportunity to entertain, learn to play with a straight bat and withstand the pressure of teasing and sledging that regularly occurred. Little wonder that when Malcolm Denzil Marshall made his debut against the Australians who are famous for this type of gamesmanship, he took it all in his stride and was unphased by it all. He had been baptised under the fire of such from his playing days with us in Queen's Park.

If the aforementioned lads such as Richard, Georgie and Moss had been able to make the transition from hopping ball to hard ball, the cricket world would have been in for a treat. They would have walked into the West Indies team with relative ease. This was proven to me when Malcolm sauntered his way into test cricket and went on to become one of the legends of the modern game, before his untimely demise.

Many a Sunday morning I witnessed those three bludgeoners of the cricket ball hammer not only Malcolm but anyone who was bold enough to run in to bowl to them. Indeed Malcolm himself was in total awe of these players and had the maximum respect for their explosive ability.

The lads of Nelson Street can boast of having been the inventors of the T-20 game long before it became the entertainment spectacle it now is. In order to get at least two games on weekdays, we would play twenty-overs-a-side games and finish two of these before the setting of the sun.

We were the first to shave the tennis ball and varnish it. This gave the ball more take-off and the batsmen had to be watchful when playing against such, as some bowlers had the uncanny ability to make these balls skid onto you from just short of a length.

Later on we experimented by taping the ball with electrical tape. This version of the game has now become somewhat of a Bajan novelty. All of this was done before 1970 by the members of the Oxley Cricket Team. That was the name of the Nelson Street team.

Nowadays all and sundry lay claim to be the inventors of these forms of cricket. But I want it to be known that I had been seeing these forms of the game while still a young lad of just thirteen years old. I firmly believe that someone must document and chronicle these happenings before the wrong person or persons step forward to accept the accolades for something that they came and found in existence.

Beach cricket was another nursing ground for applying the finishing touches to your batting and bowling technique. One of the fastest deliverers of the soft ball on the beach was Don Mandeville. He was a handful in those days and had a pace reminiscent of that tear away fast bowler from Australia Jeff Thompson.

The beach game was played on that stretch where the water surged to meet the hard wet sand, and the bowlers would bide their time in trying to deliver the ball at the appropriate occasion in order to exploit the turf for its purchase of speed. On some occasions throwing was even allowed to add to the further excitement of the game.

These were my boyhood days, and if I live to be a hundred years old I will never forget them. Today's youth sitting on street corners, peddling drugs and making their way in and out of prison will never know the joy we as young men had in participating in these games. They went a long way in building character and instilling discipline, not to mention camaraderie, a sense of fair play and respect for your fellow man.

I wouldn't trade them for all the tea in China.

Browne's Beach

Barbados is known as the land of sea and sun. It has some of the most beautiful beaches one can find anywhere on God's earth.

In my estimation there is no beach on the island that matches Browne's Beach. It has a pristine presence that acts as a perfect backdrop for the historic Carlisle Bay. In recent times its innocent emergence as a place of business and recreation has surprised no one, as this has been foreseen ages ago, but has only now come to fruition. Browne's Beach must rank among the ten best beaches in the world if not the best.

My entire life has been spent on Browne's Beach. I've used no other beach as frequently as this one. I have bathed at Miami Beach on one occasion, at Brandon's beach a similar amount and at Folkestone Beach in a half-ditched attempt.

My entire beach life has been centered in, around and way deep below Browne's Beach. I swam there, ran there, exercised there, drank, smoked, partied, slept, got high, got drunk, made love, worked, and generally lived there. Just like Nelson Street and its environs, I've known no place as intimately as I have come to comprehend this beach.

Over the years I have seen many changes occur on Browne's Beach. The social face of the beach now threatens to take on a transformation that will alienate the residents of Rebitts Land from their beloved aquatic playground.

The floundering tourist trade which had for years totally ignored Browne's Beach, has now reared its ugly head and all across its golden sands the distracting and unsightly picture of beach chairs and umbrellas has created the horrific scene of beach hustling, crime against tourists, and such other acrimonious activities not associated with a place where one would want to frequent to unwind and respect the ambiance of nature.

Now, everywhere the ever-present un-uniformed policemen and the uniformed beach rangers present sea bathers with the ungainly presence of regulative recreation. Something far removed from the tradition we had come to expect would have lasted a lifetime. It begs to wonder why before the advent of many caucasian visitors to the island, we had not seen such an attempt to police and protect Browne's Beach. It is as if these officers' one and only duty is to protect these tourists. The more things change the more they remain the same; or as my granny used to say 'The higher the monkey climbs, the more he shows his ass.'

These days my beloved Browne's Beach has become a sideshow with all and sundry joining in the act of working for the Yankee dollar (all and sundry, except for the humble folks from the Nelson Street and Rebitt's Land area). On close inspection one will realize that there are only about two inhabitants from the area who conduct their trade on this beach. Watersports operators and other beach hustlers originated from such faraway places as St. Lucy, St. James and St. Joseph. All of these have suddenly appeared on the Browne's Beach landscape, no doubt lured there by the prevalence of tourists from the various cruise liners docked in the Bridgetown Harbor.

The dichotomy of the event is one of an 'us versus them' attitude. The water operators and the beach hustlers believe that the proverbial buck must stop at them, and that they are the sole proprietors of Browne's Beach. The crumbs from off the table are left for the residents. Now a criminal element has emerged with the resulting regular skirmishes among the hustlers and incidences of tourists losing their personal belongings while they are having a bath.

This behavior has unfairly reflected poorly on the inhabitants of nearby Nelson Street and Rebitt's Land. As has always been the case, whenever some incident occurs on Browne's Beach the rest of the country is prone to wash their mouths on these unsuspecting

Beach chairs with tourists on Browne's Beach

Beach chairs outside Copacobana

Copacobana Beach Bar

people, simply on the basis of the beach being in close proximity to the said area.

There is now prevalence of idle and untrustworthy persons frequenting the beach, especially during the winter tourist season. Most of the business is transacted at this time.

Some beach bars have taken to offering the local and imported beers on special. Originally $10 BDS can purchase four bottles of brew. However, some unscrupulous felons have taken to the habit of approaching the tourists and changing the price most fraudulently to $10 US for the four beers, thereby siphoning off and pocketing a profit of ten dollars. Needless to say a rip-roaring trade is carried on with this. Local law enforcers turn a blind eye to all this practice, only interesting their investigative skills towards the arresting of the drug trade.

Long before all this corruptive behavior invaded Browne's Beach, this was a place where the Black Barbadian could enjoy a sea bath without the indignity of having to collide with these malcontents and their nefarious activities. Somehow, every time I visit Browne's Beach nowadays, I get the distinct impression that I am an intruder.

In the sixties the island was now coming out of the throes of colonialism, and independence was in the air, if not on the lips of every Bajan. Things were being done differently from the period of the planter's rule. The new political party led by the Rt. Excellent Errol

Barrow was educating the people about their rights as citizens of this emerging nation. Everyone walked with a pride and went about their daily business with an industry that was previously non-existent.

Every evening on Browne's Beach the inhabitants from the nearby Bay Land, Dunlow Lane, and Nelson Street areas gathered at the water's edge as the tiny fishing boats chugged their way to shore. With their small engines at the back, and gaily sporting their multi-colored hulls, the scene took on the appearance of a regatta of sorts as they dotted the seascape on their way towards the waiting customers.

Many persons stood patiently with plastic bags or some other container in hand and at the ready. Some small boys would be playing in the surf under the watchful eyes of the grownups in the immediate area. As soon as the first of the boats began to arrive, the grownups would order the small boys out of the water for their own safety.

As the boats neared the shore the chugging of the engines became clearer, and a single fisherman would be visible at the stern of the vessel, seemingly in battle with a long stick. This acted as a steering wheel to manipulate the rudder and kept the boat on a relatively straight course.

Many of these fishermen were of fine muscularity and their defined looks jumped out at you from beneath their clothes. Their working garb varied from fisherman to fisherman. Some preferred to use the retired tunics of the Harbor Policemen. Probably after serving their time in crime fighting, and now a little worse for wear, I believed they exchanged hands (from constable to fisherman) for a steady supply of fish as the receiving party saw fit.

The crowd would surge forward to the water's edge and make a kind of guard of honor for the arriving vessel. As soon as the boat reached the same surf, where only a few minutes ago the young boys had been playing, all hands came on deck and started to gently persuade the boat from the water up on to sand. Here another set of workers would be busy setting up a scaffolding of sorts, which consisted of old oil drums. These they fitted underneath the sides of the boat to prevent it from toppling over. Then the commotion started in earnest.

First of all, I observed that many of the men who had assisted with the docking were given several helpings of fish, and they seemed generally thankful for this compensation.

Then it was the turn of the fish sellers. What a rowdy and raucous lot they were, especially the female ones. They kept the most noise as they haggled with the captain of the boat or in some instances the owner (these were not always one and the same person) in an attempt to garner the cheapest price for the commodity.

Sometimes the language between fish seller and fisherman reached a point where the naïve would believe an altercation would soon erupt. In my young confused mind at the time, I could not perceive that these men dressed in these woolen Harbour Police uniforms were not associated with the long arm of the law. In my estimation, at any time one of these foul-mouthed individuals would be arrested and escorted off to the Main Guard, as I had heard my grandmother admonish me would have been my fate for using this colorful language.

This haggling and harangue continued until a bargain was struck and both parties were convinced that the price arrived at constituted a proper point of sale, where each could say that a profit was made. Here the count would be started, as the fish were purchased by the hundreds.

Sometimes the fish would be placed in a basket made of straw or at other times into a bucket made of zinc. The seller usually had helpers to assist with the transportation of the fish. A length of cloth was circled around the palms of their hands into something of a pad, and placed on top of their heads. Next they would ask some kind person or persons for a 'lift up'. At this point they would lower their height slightly and the helper or helpers would grab a side of the container while the fish seller grabbed the other side.

Then with one unchoreographed movement they would in tandem and with great precision lift the fully laden container on to the fish seller's padded head. She would in turn take her balance, and then assure the helpers that she was safe by issuing a loud "Thank Ya, God Bless ya." Then she would set off loudly declaring "Fish, fish! Flying fish!" and then as if just an aside she would add "Ten fuh a dollar! Ten fuh a dollar!" as she headed up out of the market and onto the streets of Bridgetown plying her trade.

From as early as four thirty in the morning, Browne's Beach comes alive. Many septuagenarians, octogenarians, and not to mention the many centenarians make their way or are assisted as is the case with the afflicted, down to the beach to take a dip. It is the most appropriate time for the locals to enjoy this tranquil and beautiful beach. At this hour the waters of Browne's Beach are crystal clear, and if one can brave the bleakness of the morning temperatures, they provide a sensation to last throughout the entire day.

One can dive among the small fish that come close to the shore at this time, and sea horses and platefish can be observed more easily, for the peacefulness is unencumbered by the irritating noises of jet-ski and motorized vessels of those in search of the illusive Yankee dollar. It is a perfect time for snorkeling, kayaking or just relaxation.

These early morning risers perform this ritual daily, and have formed a club of some kind. They inquire after each other's well being, and for the most part are their brother's keeper.

The days of my youth were a lovely time to be a part

of the Browne's Beach experience. As with the early morning risers, some older folks would invariably attend the beach at around seven or eight o'clock, and go through the same ritualistic pattern of their earlier counterparts. They would paddle in the water, exercising their muscles and freeing their joints. Intermittently, some would be in the habit of taking the water and vigorously clapping it into their joints and proudly exclaiming: "This good for the arthritis and the rheumatism."

Some others, quite adventurously, would toss a bottle into the open sea and swim out to fetch it. They would then submerge with the bottle and attempt to fill it with sea water. This water was said to have certain medicinal properties, as many boasted that ailments they had procured over the years had been cured by using this maritime medicine.

Anyone viewing these harmonious and ritualistic happenings at this time of the morning could hardly imagine the mayhem and volatile activity that would engulf the Carlisle Bay area in just a few short hours.

Long before I was born and even had entered the country, the beach had taken on a semi-apartheid complexion. The nearby Yacht Club was practicing an exclusivity that would in later times be taken over by the Harbor Lights (the Harbor Whites as it was ignobly named) and even later by the Boat Yard.

The young boys who were quite proficient at swimming and other sea games had shown an interest in learning the game of water polo. They were discouraged from such, not by the whites, but from all accounts by the black security guards, who it is said used long whips to beat back the encroaching youngsters. A wall had been erected far into the sea, as a partition to divide whites from blacks, and in some extraordinary case, rich from poor.

When Errol Barrow won the government, it is alleged that he had taken a bulldozer and broken down the wall, thus allowing the sea bathers to mingle freely on the entire stretch of beach without let or hindrance.

Nowadays fishing has been relegated to the early morning fish pot handlers. These handlers brave the coldness of the dawn to sell their catch to many of the early risers. These pot fish are sold by the pound and are quite cheap at this time of day. It is a case of the early bird catching the sweetest fish.

Fishing has given way to the tourist trade, as the fish themselves have gone to distant realms in order to escape the chaotic and noisy pleasure craft and the intrusive sail boats with their passengers.

Modern development has been cruel and yet kind to Browne's Beach. With the shifting tide, the beach itself has become wider, and the waters having receded as if expecting a tsunami to arrive at any moment. This has given rise to the scramble for beach space in order to set out beach chairs and umbrellas for the sun loving tourists. This is the bane of confusion, with the beach front owners believing that the beach and the water in front of their property are one and the same.

The hospital jetty where I learned to swim has been dismantled and taken away. However, nature has had the last laugh, for way beneath the sands of Browne's Beach lay two concrete slabs, which in earlier times were the two cornerstones for our aquatic pool. Here we spent many an hour executing our favorite moves, and generally learning sea life. Now that the jetty has been taken down, a large slice of our history has been taken away as well.

Indeed, if they could get away with it, methinks they would deem Browne's Beach a private beach. Some may disagree, but I have slowly come to see an attempt to marginalize the local user.

At one stage I was employed at the newly-renovated Copacobana Beach Bar. The manager had, in his enthusiasm to make his patrons as comfortable as possible, extended his line of chairs right up to the ebbing tide. Later in the day some youngsters had descended upon the beach for their daily game of soccer.

The tourists and their chairs had suddenly become endangered by this set of marauding brats, for want of a better word, chasing a football all around their peace and tranquility. The manager had enlisted me to stop these youngsters from playing on their beach. I, in turn, had solved the ensuing predicament in the following way.

As soon as any tourist vacated their chair and

umbrella, I inadvertently closed them down and remove the chairs into storage for the day. In a short while all the tourists had sought shelter elsewhere and all the chairs and umbrellas were removed. The youngsters now had a FIFA sized pitch to play on. The day was saved.

The hospital jetty was a permanent fixture in our lives at the time. It stood just to the south of Jemmott's Lane on Bay Street. From there one could view The Roman Catholic Church and the Old General Hospital. To the left was the old Eye Ward and on its right stood the Savoy Dance Hall, which later was to become the Child Care Board.

The jetty was made of huge slabs of timber, and was held together by large nuts and bolts. For years it had withstood the fury of the sea and remained unmovable. It was here that most of us had learned to swim, and during the summer we spent the entire day there fishing, swimming, playing cricket and football, as well as all the other things that unsupervised young people did in those days to pass the time.

Browne's Beach in this time was not as it stands today. There was an abundance of marine life to be experienced then that now no longer exists. Some may remember the days when the now almost extinct sea eggs would wash ashore, and we would break their shells and extract the raw ingredients for our consumption. Then it would be a normal occasion to witness the majesty of a school of flying fish take

The site of the old hospital jetty, now overgrown with trees

The entrance to Copacobana

flight close to shore. There is nothing left on Browne's Beach to rival this event. Then there were the sting rays which we had given the name of skeet's. Spear fishing, otherwise called 'graining', was the occupation of some of the more adventurous lads.

The spear or grain was an indigenous invention. A long piece of steel rod was used, and we would sharpen one end into a point. The gun was made of wood and the spear was held in place by rubber strands pulled taut to exact tension. When the gun was set it took on the presence of a lethal weapon, and any fish who fell on the wrong side of this instrument met with an instant death. In the local seafarers stores a more improved and finer fish gun was sold, but needless to say these were out of the range of our pockets at the time. And so necessity became the mother of our inventive minds and hands.

Sea cats, congas and barracudas were the main prey for these weapons of choice. Some other lads would sit on the jetty armed with nylon lines attached to small fish hooks. We would place any bait we could find from the nearby fish market on the hooks and toss them into the paths of the old wives, grunts and cavallies that traversed the pristine waters of Carlisle Bay. Any catch of size would be kept to enhance the pot at home. The smaller fish would alternately be recycled as bait.

To the innocent bystander who did not live in the area, these activities might have seemed as light recreation. Little did they know that the fish and sea creatures caught here would form a delicious evening meal for our poor families? The breadfruit trees on the fringe of the beach would provide us with some fibrous food to fill us, sometimes garnished with a piece of pig-tail that we sneaked out of our mother's larder, along with some Palm Tree cooking butter.

The fishermen would gratuitously provide us with a couple of flying fish and some dolphin roes. We would gather dried sticks and wood, and pretty soon a roaring fire would be ignited to cook the provisions. All on the beach, who desired, would be treated to a small nutritious meal from the communal pot; which was usually some discarded container we found on the beach. It was a life of Robinson Crusoe mixed with Treasure Island, and here we had learnt how to survive in the wild without the luxury of pots and pans, knives and forks, or any of the implements we had at home.

The old General Hospital site on Jemmotts Lane

Later on, our bellies filled with the nutritious sea food, we would embark onto the Jetty and entertain the crowd gathered there with our swimming and diving prowess.

These were the days of our youth and they would stand us in good stead as we matured, and life became somewhat meticulous with the socio-economic down turns we would face. I must sympathize with anyone who is not privileged to have had days such as these. Life as it stands now has become more of drudgery, and as the finances that we now earn can scarcely provide for our ever-increasing appetite for the exotic and expensive foods that the modern youngsters now yearn for.

When we grew tired of Browne's Beach, we would walk over to the Esso Jetty and, climbing up to the top of shed where the fishermen came to fill up their boats with diesel, we would again 'hit off' into the deep waters exhibiting our home-grown maneuvers. This time we had to be vigilant, for the Harbor Police in their boats were standing resplendent in their uniforms and ever ready to give chase. It was all in jest and no disrespect was ever meant. If all went well we would later on travel further down to the Harbor Police Station itself and engage in some table tennis, as long as we could assure the policemen on duty that we would be of proper behavior.

Like all boys, we would soon become tired of the back and forth of the table tennis, and as it would now be getting late, we moved back up past the Exchange Building (now the London Bourne Towers) and on through Waterloo Alley, where the Pondside Public Bath was situated. We would wash the sea salt from our skins in the male section, listening intently to hear any of the females on the other side as they went about their bathing. Mischievously we would creep silently up the walls of our side and take in an eyeful of the naked ladies on the other side, until we were caught, or one of us had given away our position. At this point all hell would break loose, as the women would curse us for our inquisitiveness. Some, however, would find distinct pleasure in displaying all the goods for us to behold. As young boys this would prove too much, and we would scamper away giggling at having seen the flowers in bloom.

All in all I can say that these days helped to provide us with the necessary rites of passage as young men to enable us to go on to become real men. Again I must declare that these were days that I would not trade for all the fish in the sea.

Now that Browne's Beach has become a haven for the rich and famous and a hunting ground for hustlers and pilferers, I thank God that, along with my friends, I was given the privilege to experience this slice of heaven right here on earth.

Gone are the flying fish in all their majesty, the sea eggs are no more, the skeets, the congas, the sea cats, the old wives and cavallies have all migrated to other places. The Hospital Jetty, the Esso Jetty, the Harbor Police Station and its jetty have all been demolished, and now all that remains are the exclusive night clubs and restaurants that seek to deny the inhabitants of Rebitt's Land entry to their establishments. The only remaining glory is Doris' Beach Bar. This is an indigenous place of entertainment for the poor of Bridgetown. This is owned by a St. Lucian Lady who goes affectionately by the name of Doris. Only God knows how much longer she has to live, but heaven help the poor people of the city if this bar is taken over by those who seek to only cater to the tourists. Then they will have the opportunity to erase the poor man from the beachfront that may have been his for all eternity.

In Golden Square with the Slingers

Dusk time was approaching with the swiftness of a hundred meters sprinter. The neighborhood boys were conducting a game of dice under the street light which stood like a sentry in the middle of Golden Square.

Golden Square was the starting point of the 1937 riots. It is located on the spot where the Bridgetown Plaza was situated. Before the Cinema stood there, Golden Square was a meeting point for the wannabe trade unionists and politicians of the day. National Hero Clement Osbourne Payne had taken a liking to the area and set about hosting meetings there. He became endeared to the humble folks of Golden Square. It was at Golden Square that the famous statement that had allegedly given signal of happenings to come: "Today is a funny night."

Oftentimes I believe that these events have led Rebitt's Land and Nelson Street to bear the brunt of the island's wrath for being the launching pad for social change in the country. I also believe that this stigmatization exists because of the colonial Barbadian's thrust to be seen as always on the side of the planter classes. They have always held them in a revered status despite the atrocities enacted against them by these slave masters. Having been backed into a corner through fear more than anything else they have remained steadfast in their support for their oppressors.

These events had provided the rest of the island with one more reason to dislike the Nelson Street men. But there were other reasons for the disdain that contemporary Barbadians had for these unsuspecting individuals.

Never mind the riots had caused the masters in Britain to sit up and take notice of the plight of those of the lower socio-economic bracket. The die would be cast, for almost one hundred years Nelson Street was to be avoided at all costs, and minimal contact if any was to be made with anyone living there.

This state of affairs has led the inhabitants to acquire an inferiority complex when compared to other people throughout the island.

Bets were flying to and fro and one of the players had been throwing the dice for the last forty-five minutes without cutting out. Backing every single point, he was on top of the game, as indicated by the rising pile of Eastern Caribbean currency rapidly accumulating

Golden Square with the monument commemorating the 1937 riots

Bust of Clement Payne

in front of him. Some were placing outside bets on his throwing, obviously impressed by either his prowess or his available fortune.

Every now and then the boys would glance over their shoulders as if in anticipation of the arrival of some uninvited guest. On one such occasion one of the boy's remarked.

"I tell wunna fuhget bout he. This time he somewhere picking a fare."

"You en know you does talk bare shite?" One older boy, who went by the name of Chippy-O, replied. "A big able police officer of the law in a club picking fares?" Chippy-O asked.

"So because he is a police, dah mean he don't like woman?" The first boy countered.

"Fool yuhself wid dah then." Chippy-O was not one to give in easily to an argument, and many were beginning to surmise that as he got older he was prone to become more and more miserable than before.

A voluptuous young girl passed on the opposite side of the road, pretending she hadn't seen the boys.

"Hello darling. You look so lovely today. One of the young Casanovas offered.

"Guh long sweetie, doan find nuh talk fuh he. He just come out a jail," one of his friends joked, and the boys burst out laughing.

The girl, believing that they were laughing at her, pouted her lips and started strutting provocatively down the lane. This caused both entities of her rear end to jiggle merrily as if in tune to some calypso only she could hear.

The boys were delighted.

"Shake it baby, shake it. Ya muddah tek nine months to make it, so shake it but doan break it." This time Freddie Simmons was the speaker.

Of all the boys in Golden Square, Freddie was the most revered. His grandmother was the owner of a bakery on Nelson Street and this had made him a celebrity of sorts. The young girls adored him with the adulation young adolescent girls have for older boys, along with his ability with words and his known affinity with the opposite sex.

"Freddie come here a minute," the young girl pleaded.

"You can't see I gambling?" Freddie said in as soft a voice as he could muster. "You know it does bring bad luck to interrupt a game when it in progress?"

"So talking to me is bad luck now? Okay, Freddie, Okay!"

"Darling doan get on so, you know when I done here all my time for you honey."

Freddie was vigorously fighting his case, not wanting to surrender his manhood to this Bajan hot spot in the presence of his friends, but at the same time not wanting to be in the young lady's bad books any time soon.

"Still going to the dance to night with me?" Freddie asked hopefully.

"You want me to go?" she inquired.

These young men were besides themselves, and brimming with confidence. They literally had most of the young girls eating from the palms of their hands. They went by a sobriquet that described their powers of attraction. These were the Slingers.

In a few short years from now most of these slingers would be sowing their oats in such far out places as Australia, Mombasa, South Africa, London, Liverpool, Vancouver, California and every part of the Caribbean and South America. By this time they would have joined the ranks of the Harrison Line, the Act Boats, the Booth Line and Star Ships. They would be the emerging economic power to take Nelson Street by storm if not by surprise. They were to become the seamen. But they never relinquished their title of 'The Slingers'.

Every Old Years night Day Sue would bring out his annual Slingers list. This accounted for the first one hundred Slingers, and one had to validate their appearance on this list by showing proof of the number of girls they had bedded during the year.

Day Sue elected to become the author of this list to make sure of a top ten placing for himself. There were two places on the list that were certain, and these were the number one position and the hundredth spot. The number one spot always belonged to Courcey. The hundredth position belonged to none other than Chippy-O. It was rumored that Chippy-O was a virgin.

They said that his only chance of being laid was lost when he had succumbed to the falling temperatures of the Garrison Savannah one night.

Chippy-O had been spotted by a lass from the Bayland area one night at a dance being held at the Drill Hall, the place that now houses the Barbados Defence Force headquarters. Fredrica had asked Chippy to accompany her outside to the nearby Garrison pasture for a walk. Chippy had capitulated after much beseeching from Fredrica.

On reaching the Garrison Fredrica had become the aggressor and Chippy literally caught cold feet, and announced to Fredrica: "I gine back inside my botsee too cold out here."

Whenever this story was replayed in the presence of Chippy-O, he would become enraged and start mouthing expletives on rapid.

There is another story which Chippy had held in much trepidation, if not for the jocularity of the event, then for the inaccuracy of the anecdote. Chippy had been a prolific dancer. He could dance to any genre of music. Indeed the ladies preferred to dance with him. For besides being a good dancer, he was also a very snazzy dresser, who made many a younger version of his gender ashamed when he made his appearance on dance nights. The ladies also liked the way that he smelled. As an escort Chippy was the perfect match. But as far as the ladies were concerned, that was all there was to him, as he seemed disinterested in forming any relationships of the intimate kind.

Chippy had travelled to the country area to attend a dance given by one of his workmates at the Bridgetown Screw Dock in Cavans Lane. As soon as he had landed at the dance house, he immediately took in the dance area in search of a dancing partner.

One of the local bad-johns had left his date to go in search of refreshments. Chippy, seizing the opportunity, had stepped forward and asked for a dance with the absent bad-john's girl. She in turn, after perusing Chippy from head to toe and finding him pleasant enough to be her dancing partner, had obliged.

Chippy quickly became engrossed in the dance with this fair damsel, quite oblivious to the fact that she was already taken. The bad-john returned and was none too pleased with what he was seeing. By now Chippy and the young lady in question were wrapped together like two peas in a pod.

The bad-john quietly stepped over to Chippy, tapped him on his shoulder, and declared: Young man, you dancing too close!"

Without even looking back to view his speaker, Chippy boldly replied: "Boy, go under the cellar and dance with the cats and the dogs, when you see big people dancing," all the while skillfully navigating his partner across the dance floor.

The bad-john stormed out of the dance and returned in quick time armed with a bull pestle. He then proceeded to introduce this to Chippy's back with such ferocity that Chippy held on to the young lady and soothingly reassured her: "Sweet heart, like they pelting bottles inside a here." By this time the bad-john had made the bull pestle become further acquainted with Chippy's back, completely destroying his terylene shirt. "But don't bother bout that baby, I got you covered none can't hit you." Chippy reassured the poor lass.

Just as soon as the young girl passed, a scampering of sorts was heard and the metallic click of boots came pounding down the lane. Every man rose and turned in time to see Tom Paine the Harbor Policeman riding his bicycle full pelt towards them. By this time the game was in full swing and the dividends were plentiful. Tom Paine came, with upraised club and shouting at the top of his voice. The boys, seeing impending doom coming their way, simultaneously made the same decision and off they went in as many different directions as could confuse this aquatic policeman.

Tom Paine, seeing that his kingdom had come, decided that his will be also done and pretending to chase after the boys, he pulled up by the abandoned cash and proceeded to help himself to all of it. Stuffing it into the pockets of his woolen uniform, he made good with his ill-gotten bounty.

Now he could buy himself a shot of strong rum and take home the rest to share with his wife and family.

The youngsters made their way onto Nelson Street and entered Ashby Alley and emptied out onto Beckwith Street, turning onto Spruce Street then diverting through the Concrete where they proceeded to bathe their musky bodies. Tonight there would be a dance in Queen's Park, and every boy would be there trying to seduce the female offerings there. The St. Lucians and the Dominicans would be out in full effect, dressed in their Sunday-go-to-meetings. The Slingers would ply their romantic prowess in an effort to pull one of these island beauties.

After taking their baths in the Concrete public bath, the slingers would make their separate ways to their separate homes and get dressed. In a couple of minutes these wild boys would be virtually unrecognizable as they strutted with poise and swagger, clad in the latest styles and carrying the scents of the movies stars and the rich and famous.

It was the twenty sixth of December. The night after Christmas, normally called Boxing Day. It was also the date of the annual dance of Bob the Bearded Sweetsman, held at the Queen's Park Steel Shed. He was a sweets seller who plied his wares on Swan Street. His dance was a staple on the Christmas list of things to do.

Queen's Park on Christmas morning after Church to display formal wear and Bob's dance on Boxing Day where casual fashion was the order of the night. One dared not repeat the clothes from Christmas morning to Bob's dance. This would ensure that your name would be the talking point the next day.

Everyone who was someone would be there. A local hi-fi man provided the musical entertainment, and the fashions of the season were all on display for the roving eyes of the fashionistas to peruse and critique.

The Nelson Street crew would be out in full effect, dressed to kill in their debonair threads. The seamen were the talk of the town and the catch of the night for the women. Many a man had lost his woman on a night such as this to one the seafarers, not to mention the young brigade from Golden Square.

The Head Cornerstone

As has been shown before, the area has produced many illustrious sons and daughters, who have carved a niche for themselves throughout the Barbadian landscape. They have gone on against all the odds and the most humble and humiliating of beginnings to achieve success in their chosen fields.

Over a period of time the Guyanese have somewhat become ingrained into the social landscape of the area. Some of them have taken the liberty to enter into the commercial activity of the area. The legal side, that is.

One woman readily comes to mind. After having made her advent into the whore trade, she has emerged as the largest property and business owner in the area.

Xenophobia reared its ugly head a few years ago in the area. This was set off with the arrival of some sex workers from the Albouyce Town area in Georgetown.

They seemed to have a particular grouse with the Nelson Street area and its inhabitants.

A couple of altercations ensued, and the end result was that the immigration authorities were notified of this malfeasance and the potentially dangerous situation that prevailed. Pretty soon the authorities descended upon Nelson Street one night and rounded up the offending parties. Much later a more pleasant crew of ladies arrived. They made friends with the locals and were welcomed into the area.

In recent times the immigration has eased up somewhat, and the GT's (Guyanese) have shown that they have a role to play in our small society.

As has been mentioned before, one of the biggest property owners in the Red Light District is a Guyanese. She has had the foresight to buy her own properties and rebuild them. She has made a complex of sorts in the Golden Square/Jordan lane vicinity, complete with hair salon and barbershop, as well as a dance hall area. She also runs a Wholesale Drinks depot that services almost all of Greater Bridgetown. The Guyanese have shown their propensity for business, and are no longer viewed as just being on the island to rob Bajans of their jobs and their men.

The Guyanese know how to celebrate and throw a party. Recently, a most unfortunate incident occurred between a Barbadian lad and his Guyanese mate, resulting in the death of the Guyanese boy. In what could have become a volatile situation, the residents of Nelson Street rallied around the family of the bereaved, and held a candle light vigil in the area for the slain lad.

This was a most unfortunate incident, as the two boys were good friends, but a little argument got way out of hand and with tempers raging. There was no attempt at conflict resolution and what could have been written off as a juvenile spat wounded up with the death of a youngster still in the prime of his life. It was a dark hour in the lives of the Folks of Nelson Street. Even the mother of the perpetrator showed up to lend support to the family in their time of grief.

The other factor that in my opinion has enabled the population of Barbados to practice their discrimination against the people of Rebitt's Land and Nelson Street is the one where history records that Nelson Street and nearby Fairchild Street were the first two communities on the island to be affected by the cholera outbreak of the 1800s. It is this coupled with the fact that sanitation standards in this neglected area were of a poor quality, even for the period.

This state of affairs has led the inhabitants to accept an inferiority complex as a permanent fixture on their social resume.

Prostitution has always been the mainstay of the commercial activity in the area. Working under the adage of "who has the money can get the pussy and who has the pussy can make the money." The 'bread and sweat of thy brow' policy of the area can be literally said to be enacted on one's back with some dauntless bumpkin perched on top, grunting and groaning on his way to a shuddering climax. And all this is for the acquisition of legal tender for the payment of any amount.

The title of whores and thieves has been upgraded from the ignoble publicans and sinners. This was the statement that had given reason for the construction of St. Ambrose Church.

Sex workers on Nelson Street are for the most part imported. Any Bajans working there in this profession can scarcely be said to boast of having their navel string buried in Barbados.

Guyanese make up the most of these, followed by Jamaicans and those from the Dominican Republic. There was a time when Trinidad and Tobago had provided the backbone for this trade. In recent times their numbers have dwindled to the extent that the presence of a Trini sex worker is now somewhat of a novelty.

The area of Golden Square is historically, socially and politically charged, as one of the most militant and culturally potent in the Southern Caribbean. Now the defunct Fairchild market has been relocated on the spot where the Bridgetown Plaza was once housed, before it fell victim to the ravages of fire.

On the spot is a bust of National hero the Rt. Excellent Clement Osbourne Payne. He was a political agitator who was the catalyst behind the 1937 riots. Once again wisdom can be found in the strangest of places, for it was these riots that made the colonial masters sit up and take notice of the horrendous conditions of living throughout the entire island at the time.

The stone that the builders refused had now become the head cornerstone.

Images of Redemption

You have to believe in yourself when no one else does. that's what makes you a winner

Venus Williams

If you want to be acceptable to others you first have to be acceptable to yourself

Malcolm X

If life gives you a lemon, squeeze it and make lemonade.

Anonymous

It can be said with proficient accuracy that no politician has ever lifted one finger to help the plight of the good folks of Nelson Street. They have for decades been exploited for their votes and promise after promise has gone unfulfilled.

Indeed one can offer a case for Dame Billie Miller. She can point to the Bridgetown Sewerage Project as the saving grace for the area from becoming one of dereliction and unsanitary surroundings. She had a vision for the entire city, but her somewhat early retirement has curtailed her drive to make Bridgetown a fully vibrant city.

None other has done anything else but massage the people in the procurement of electoral votes. Some of them seem to think that their presence at funerals and candle-light vigils for deceased persons of the area is the zenith of their duties. They then continue to neglect the residents and their pleas for social amenities. As we speak there is no Community Resource Centre in the area.

An indication of the insensitivity of the authorities for the area is evidenced by the erection of a basketball court in a populace that is predominantly occupied with soccer. Any useful demographic test would have proven that in the Nelson Street area there are few if any basketball players. With no meaningful program at work, this court, minus the resource centre, seems to me as only a token of appreciation from some politician in an effort to cajole the electorate that they have the best interest of the people at heart.

The police have developed a bias against the youth of the area, all of this because of the drug trade. Not all of the youth are involved in the drug trade, and the few who are only do so for lack of any meaningful alternative. However, this does not sit well with the lawmen. They turn up in the area, guns at the ready, as if they are there to apprehend some dangerous criminal.

On one occasion I witnessed a squad of Task Force officers armed to the teeth invade the home of a lactating mother. What made this incident stand out in my memory is the fact that a couple of female officers were present, and they proceeded to view the poor mother with scorn, as if she was some dirty object.

When the neighbors reacted in her defense, they were threatened with beatings and arrest. Meanwhile the toddler, so rudely interrupted from his evening meal started to cry. One would have thought that this alone would have made the officers more sympathetic and humane. But no such luck.

These servants of the law who are sworn to serve and protect the good citizens of Barbados reminded me that evening of accounts I have heard and read about the Nazi Gestapo in the Second World War during their persecution of the Jews. It might sound a bit farfetched, but that's the impression I was given by these goose-stepping law enforcers. What compounds the nonsensical escapade was the fact that nothing was found on the premises of the woman. The hoodlums then left the area without so much as an apology for their actions.

Such is the disdain that law and order have for the residents of Nelson Street.

Now let's go to the malfeasance of the criminals. Everyone uses Nelson Street as their hideout spot after they have committed a crime. Many a wanted person has made the area their haven, and show scant respect for the inhabitants and their innocent offspring. Some of them even threaten the folks with action if it can be ascertained that they have given information to the Police about their whereabouts.

Therefore as can be clearly seen, there is no respite for the Rebitterians from either the law authorities or the criminals, and there is no respect.

Nothing gets attention faster than demonizing a person. The people of Nelson Street have been demonized as being lazy and dysfunctional. Nothing can be further from the truth. This is only an excuse to portray them as welfare seekers.

People on welfare want desperately to get off. Have you ever visited the offices of the Welfare Department? There is an unbearable stench that pervades the compound. It is the stench of poverty. The same one carried by vagrants, miscreants, addicts, garbage trucks and landfill dumps. No one in their right senses would want to be a part of such for their entire life. But if better can't be done then the children have to be fed.

The children of the area have lifted the spirits of the elders with their talents and skills. Many of them have performed quite well in the 11 plus examinations, and have attained passes to some of the more affluent schools on the island. This is in itself a credit to the ministrations of the teachers of St. Ambrose School. The crack addicts of the Oxley Street area had at one time held both teachers and pupils literally hostage in their own classrooms with the ever-present scent of crack cocaine, as they carried out their deadly practice right under the noses of the poor children and teachers.

After many protestations, the powers that be heard the cries of the school. Subsequently the children were temporarily moved to the premises of the old Bishop's Court, and a new and improved state of the art school was constructed on the site of the former one. With improved security, the new school is now a beacon for any primary school to follow. The crackheads have now resorted to the nearby St. Ambrose Centre to use and sell the deadly cocaine.

So from out of adversity has arisen a new sense of purpose for the school. The paros, as they are called can no longer interfere with the daily running of this learning institution and the children themselves have a brand new complex where they can feel safe.

While on the subject of the children of St. Ambrose School, I must make reference to an incident I observed some eleven years ago.

I was a member of the Contenders Calypso Tent at the time, and we were invited by the Caribbean Broadcasting Corporation to attend their annual Festival Stage program. The event was held on the grounds at the headquarters of the corporation, beneath some tents. When we arrived we saw some small children from the St. Ambrose School. Many of them instantly recognized me and we started a rapport of sorts. The children were displaying good behavior and proper deportment. At one stage radio personality Mr. Tony Thompson walked under the tent where the guests were seated and announced to the children "Good Morning Children". The children replied in unison "Good Morning Sir," and surprised everyone with their additional "How are you doing this morning?" This caused the dignitaries and guests to applaud.

Two prominent female broadcasters were seated right behind me, one of them being the CEO of the Corporation at the time. They were generally impressed with the manners and behavior of the children.

They wanted to know the name of the school and where it was from. They had observed that many of the children were familiar with me and proceeded to inquire of me the name and the location of the school.

I informed them that the name of the school was the St. Ambrose School and that it was situated in the Nelson Street area. They appeared dubious at first, and I overheard one lady remark "Oh, he doesn't know where they are from either."

I decided to hold my peace. and declined to take her up on her inclination to believe that children of such impeccable and impressive manners could not be from the Nelson Street area.

In a while one of the teachers arrived on the scene, and the ladies, feeling confident that they would now discover the identity of the school and its location , asked the same question of the teacher that they had asked of me .

When the teacher in question had replicated the answer I had already given, I noticed a kind of hush fell among the ladies for a while. After a few seconds one of them broke the silence and tapped me on my shoulder to lay her opinion.

"Who would have believed that, huh?"

I smiled. The future of Nelson Street had saved the day. There was indeed hope; images of redemption in the face of the social exclusion.

Ever since that day I had resolved that if it was the last thing I did on this earth, I would document and chronicle the Nelson Street that I know and have come to love dearly, If only to give credence to the self-worth of these excluded folk.

About the Author

Christopher David Alleyne was born in Paddington, London. His Barbadian mother and Nigerian father provided the cultural diversity that has been the mainstay of his creativity.

At the age of 4 he was sent to Barbados to live with his grandparents and his uncle. He received his education there and earned the nickname of 'Scotty' from his classmates, who couldn't believe he was born in England, and insisted that it had to be Scotland. Such was the train of thought in Barbados at the time.

He attended the Bay Primary School up to the age of 10 when he won a place at the prestigious Combermere

School. It was here that one of his English teachers (none other than the legendary Timothy Callender) discovered his writing skills and encouraged him to enhance them by becoming an avid reader.

Upon leaving school he did a short stint as a Public Health Inspector in the southern parishes of the country. He soon grew frustrated with the politics of the Bajan Civil Service, and exited to join the ranks of the Canadian Farm Labour Scheme where he spent two years.

In later years he decided to return to his birthplace after some 54 years on Barbadian soil.

This is his first book, a lifelong dream.

Made in the USA
Columbia, SC
03 August 2017